Comment

This paperback copy of ''Religions and History'' was originally assembled for classroom study in a non-sectarian, independent school. It paralleled instruction in the Senior classes in American History.

Selected for study and continuing review were eleven current, newsworthy religions. The list could be expanded arbitrarily if world conditions merited attention.

This study reveals mankind's endless search for a Power greater than his own. Now and then, failing in such quest, man nominated himself as the epitome of an evolutionary process, deistically unrelated, but inviting spacial research.

Any contemporary historical look at the United States of America reveals a population background which is predominantly Christian in origin, worship practice, and religious commonality – despite the historical background of the American Indian and several centuries of immigration from non-Christian cultures.

''Religions and History'' was not designed as a missionary effort to expand the number of the faithful. What America is today in world history is certain to reflect the impact of its motivation upon all other political societies. Conversely, to avoid the historical religious study of other earth dwellers is to walk in darkness.

RELIGIONS AND HISTORY

RELIGIONS AND HISTORY

A Textbook for the Enlightenment of Twelfth-Graders in Our Tax-supported Public High Schools

Leslie R. Severinghaus

Preface by Henry Luce III
Introduction by Clare Boothe Luce

An Appeal To Readers

It is hoped that, without re-editing the numerical figures of the First Edition, the reader will secure a copy of the ''World Almanac'' of most recent date and make such changes as seem significant.

Incidentally, the substitution of figure changes can become a rewarding educational experience.

A PAPERBACK RENDITION

OF

RELIGIONS AND HISTORY

1991

FIRST EDITION

All rights reserved, including the right of reproduction in whole or in part in any form.

Copyright © 1986 by Leslie R. Severinghaus

Manufactured in the United States of America
ISBN: 0-533-06577-1

Library of Congress Catalog Card No.: 85-90048

To my wife, Emmavail Luce Severinghaus,
without whose lifelong inspiration
this book would not have been possible

Contents

Foreword

This textbook carries a message to the young men and women enrolled in their last year of secondary education in our high schools. At my advanced age, I think of them as boys and girls; realistically, I know that they are on the threshold of responsible adulthood. Soon they will become candidates for the job market, for specialized vocational training, or for higher education on the campuses of our colleges and universities.

In our multireligious and multiracial society are to be found virtually all religious traditions now extant throughout the continents of the world. Predominantly Christian though we are, temples, shrines, mosques, and synagogues dot our fair landscape from coast to coast and from border to border as they do also in Alaska, Hawaii, and outlying protectorates. Freely their members practice and propagate their diverse faiths, quietly rejoicing in the assurance of freedom to worship as explicitly set forth in the Constitution of the United States of America:

> Congress shall make no law respecting an establishment of religion, or prohibiting the free exercise thereof; or abridging the freedom of speech, or of the press; or the right of the people peaceably to assemble, and to petition the government for a redress of grievances.

Not elsewhere on this earth is there a nation of such geographical extent and population—230,000,000 people—where "government of the people, by the people, for the people" is a demonstrable reality. The Founding Fathers—well deserving of capitalization—were determined that in launching our democratic government, no single established church or religious order should dictate the acts of the people's government.

Consider the inscription that ennobles the Statue of Liberty at the entrance to New York's harbor. One hundred and twenty years after the Declaration of Independence, it bore testimony under the presidency of William McKinley that the lamp of Judeo-Christian brotherhood still burned brightly.

> Give me your tired, your poor, your huddled masses yearning to be free; the wretched masses from your teeming shore. Send these, the homeless, tempest-tossed to me. I lift my lamp beside the golden door.

Was that dedicatory invitation nothing more than the emotional enthusiasm of a fledgling nation designed to impress the older nations of the world? Never so! The same gratitude that moved the Pilgrim Fathers to thanksgiving for their deliverance from oppression still welled up in the hearts of God-committed Americans. Although by 1896 the population of our country had grown from 5,308,483 in 1800 to 75,994,575* in 1900, the obligation of brotherhood, instilled by Christian faith, guided the lives and thoughts of Americans. They were "their brothers' keepers."

Today's population figure of roughly 230,000,000 thus includes the birthright American children of nearly 50,000,000 immigrants who came to our shores during our 210 years of nationhood. Surely those figures are indeed unique in world history. Despite this enlargement in population count, however, the fact is verifiable that about 93 percent of all children in our public schools come from families of Christian background. The others are Jews, Moslems, Buddhists, Hindus, Confucianists, Shintoists, et cetera. It is their families who have built the temples, shrines, mosques, and synagogues where these thousands may worship in security from governmental interference.

It seems entirely reasonable, therefore, to include in our high school courses in American history—along with "taxation without representation" and other political complaints—the story of a religious heritage without which the Statue of Liberty might never have taken its stand at the "golden door" of New York's harbor. In no sense can this be interpreted as an attempt by Christianity to proselytize among other faiths, or to be a violation of the injunction to keep "church" separate from "state." That separation was accomplished once and for all time by the Founding Fathers' insertion of the First Amendment to our Constitution—that no established order of a particular creed should ever interfere with the governmental actions of the new democracy.

*U.S. Census Figures

To speak more in the contemporary idiom, although religious beliefs in America can be construed as a segment of the competitive, free enterprise system, religion remains a very personal experience. As man does, so is he seen to be. All religious people in America are free not only to worship but also "to let their light so shine" that others may pass judgment on the values by which they live. Out of this experience comes the personal commitment that each individual ultimately makes. This has nothing to do with "separation of church from state."

It is to be expected that all elected representatives in government, from township to the presidency, will contribute to this functioning democracy personal judgments that reflect the moral precepts by which they live. Even the secular humanists have the remarkable privilege of worshiping man as the highest point in evolutionary development rather than extolling a Supreme Being. What is unthinkable, however, is that we, a demonstrably Christian nation in founding and pursuant acts, should fail to give religion its rightful place in the teaching of American history. All other religious faiths, here resident, have both the privilege and the obligation to present their beliefs to their children. Only in the "free world" does this opportunity exist.

Words of caution are in order: those qualified to teach such a course in American history will be difficult to find. They must possess not only an extraordinary commitment to teaching as a profession but also a disciplined objectivity that will deny access to personal beliefs and prejudices. Let us not underestimate the learning capacities and desires of our high school seniors. History, languages, and literature come alive when taught in conjunction with a course in comparative religions.

Somehow we must do a better job of educating in our public schools lest we mindlessly steal from our young people knowledge of the great constants of life wherever they may be found. Only through our own neglect need the "American Dream" become but another example of an extinct species.

Preface

So much of what we read in popular histories and school history texts concerns itself with kings and conquerors, palaces and parliaments, trade and treaties, wars and disasters, that the enormous impact of religions on events often seems underplayed. One reason may be that we study more history that is near in time and place rather than that of the long-ago and faraway. Thus we may be more familiar with the victory of General Thomas at Chickamauga than with the evangelizing of St. Thomas on the Malabar coast.

Another reason may be that the founders of most of the great religions are seen as moralists rather than as men of action who changed political maps in their lifetimes. This, of course, is to lose sight of the fact that their influence spread widely and persisted over millennia so that it has affected political maps to this day. Still another reason is that writers and teachers of general history see their franchise as emphasizing the political and social, while relegating religion to a separate compartment.

It is obvious, however, that the interaction of religion with all human forces has been pervasive, a fact which meaningful and accurate history cannot ignore.

A study of history requires that we recognize great differences between the major thrusts of the great religions: Christianity as evangelical, Islam as warlike, Buddhism as passive, Judaism as nationalistic, but at the same time acknowledge that they represent a common human imperative, which is that some supernatural force guides our existence and future. In no case have the followers of these religions always been true to their ideals, but over time religious commitment has exercised a powerful restraint on the evils of human nature.

And so a study of history also requires that we contemplate the possibility of a Divine Being who was Creator of life and remains our Great Guide in history.

In addition, religions have often been the carriers of civilization and its cultural attributes from one area to another. Thus Buddhist monks brought a written language to an illiterate medieval Japan, enabling the Japanese for the first time to start recording their own history. And thus did Middle Eastern Moslems bring Islamic architecture and Arabic computation to India. In more recent eras, Christian missionaries have spread the knowledge of Western higher learning and modern technology throughout the world.

In this book, Leslie Severinghaus makes this case by surveying the rise of religions over the 7,500 years of recorded history. He marshalls a fascinating array of often unfamiliar statistics to show, religion by religion, and country by country, where the world stands today and how it got there. Dr. Severinghaus brings to this work the experience of some sixty years of teaching, starting in China where the confrontation of different religious traditions was enlightening and challenging. I hope *Religions and History* will be a stimulator for further research as it is intended to be.

Henry Luce III
Oyster Bay, NY, June 1985

xiv

Introduction

History is the record of man's spiritual voyage through time and space to discover the parameters of his own true nature. In my youth, the world of Christianity, built on the ruins of the Greco-Roman civilization, extended from the oriental frontiers of Russia to the Pacific shores of North and South America. That was what religious folk called "Christendom" and historians called "Western Civilization."

Christendom was flanked on the east by the lands of Buddha, Laotse, and Confucius. It covered the entire Orient.

The world of Islam ran from Pakistan to the farthest edge of Morocco, and in Africa extended nearly to the Equator.

The return in 1947, after 2000 years, of the exiled sons of Moses to Israel has produced that present day disruption in the fabric of Moslem civilization which we now call the Middle East Crisis.

History, to offer my own definition, is the story of man's search for the *Meaning of Man* and his relation to the infinite universe.

It is my high pleasure to commend for study by young Americans this story of the inescapable linkage between man's political history and his religions.

Clare Boothe Luce

RELIGIONS AND HISTORY

Chapter I

Have We Dropped Something
When No One Was Paying Attention?

"Dear Reader"—That's the way in which Victorian essayists greeted the limited number of readers whose schooling had been adequate to encourage general reading. In Colonial days, minimum literacy was sufficient to carry on the work of farm, factory, and village store. The children learned their ABCs either from their parents or from the informal groups working under the auspices of the village church. Even President Abraham Lincoln, eighty-five years later, had never heard of tax-supported public schools.

First off, let me urge you to read the foreword of this book. It may help you to accept cheerfully the requirement of yet another book for your already overcrowded bookbag! Now to the business at hand!

As members of the senior class, you have been studying the Constitution of the United States, an admirable document. You have doubtless become aware that the word *education* does not appear either in its principal text or in the subsequent amendments to the Bill of Rights. Our forefathers had left the education of the children as the special responsibility of the several states, recognizing the reasonableness of states' rights as an element of democratic government. You who sit in this classroom are a tiny but very important segment of more than 13,000,000 high school students currently being educated in the United States. As seniors anticipating graduation, you number more than 3,000,000.

The statistics provided by the National Center for Education of the U.S. Department of Education do not list a single high school graduate for 1870. In 1917, when this writer was graduated from the one high school in Wheeling, West Virginia, only 200,000 seniors, nation-wide, received diplomas. Today, sixty-nine years later, fifteen times that number will adjust their mortarboards, don flowing gowns, and proudly display their diplomas to thousands of parents and relatives in garden receptions.

That's quite an astounding accomplishment, isn't it?—from not one graduate in 1870, to more than 3,000,000 in 1985. Just how did this come to pass? The story is a complicated one. The American public school grew up something like the legendary "Topsy" who frequently played with friend "Turvy." Both financial support and curricular content varied widely from state to state. Why don't you drop in to your school library and look in the latest *World Almanac* for the ranking of the fifty states with respect to their annual expenditures for education. Find out where your state stands.

When my father attended a community log-cabin school in Indiana in 1871, he had to memorize only thirty-six states. He tells of a time when all children were kept home from school because two panthers had been seen roaming through the woods through which the children had to walk to school. To the west still lay that incredible expanse of plains, deserts, and snow-covered mountains. The Conestoga wagons still moved in long lines across the prairies. At night, the open fires lighted the faces of men, women, and children who knelt to ask God's care and protection.

When I was seven years old and reading from McGuffey's *Second Reader*, there were forty-five states to be memorized. The panthers were gone, and I was, in measured years, closer to "Custer's Last Stand" than you are to World War II!

Perhaps you haven't realized that the federal government in Washington looks upon education in an advisory capacity only, sharing its tax receipts with states in need of financial help. In addition to state management of education, quite a number of organizations, independent of both state and central government, carry on accrediting procedures on educational performance, organize teachers into labor unions, analyze testing procedures to determine student achievement, and subsist financially on the fees paid by participating people and institutions. With "so many cooks in the kitchen," is it to be wondered that the machinery of education occasionally squeaks? That is one of the acceptable penalities of "government of the people, by the people, and for the people." We wouldn't want it any other way.

Seated in contemplative mood in the impressive chambers of the Supreme Court of the United States are nine justices, all presidential appointees, whose duty it is to keep watch over the laws passed by Congress, state and local governments lest they contravene the purposes and provisions of the Constitution. Their function is not to make laws, but to ponder the problems so emerging. Their function is thus interpretive rather than creative.

The recently, much-publicized confrontation between the supporters of the theories of "evolution" and "scientific creationism" was but a continuation of a succession of such contests, variously adjudicated in our courts of law, from the lowliest level of the magistrate or town meeting, through state and lower level federal decisions, and ending as the final point of decision with the U.S. Supreme Court. In this book, our interest centers in the legal decisions respecting that perpetual stumbling block—the "separation of church and state." The problem appears to be in extraordinarily good health and promises to be with us for the foreseeable future!

What is incomprehensible to most people is our failure to recognize the utter simplicity of the forefathers' provision. Let no single, organized religious body endow itself with the power to dictate the governmental acts of the enfranchised citizens of the democracy. If the Congress of the United States wishes to continue to open its sessions with a Judeo-Christian chaplain's comforting words, so be it. We are still a Christian nation—a government of, by, and for the people. If, under the authority of the Constitution, our citizens wish to celebrate a variety of religious traditions among the children in our public, tax-supported schools, let the crèches stand in front of the buildings; let the Esquimaux erect a totem pole on the football field; let the Moslem children roll out their prayer rugs in the direction of Mecca; let the Torah enthusiasts honor their scriptures—so long as it is done in free time. Let us live up to our Christian heritage and display the love for all mankind that is basic to our Christian teachings. If we, as a Christian nation, wish to demonstrate our belief in the Gospel of Love, how can we deny this freedom of worship to others? Let them chant, ring bells, spread incense, light candles, march peacefully with their impedimenta, and send greeting cards to one another on festive occasions or holy days.

And isn't it about time that we stop assembling our state and federal judges to decide whether or not a page in the high school yearbook should be excised before distribution because it pictures the activities of a school's Bible club? Why should there not also be a Koran Club, a Buddhist Society, a Sephardic Association, an Atheist Gathering, or a Society of Christian Athletes if there is a constituency in school or college with enough fervor to institute such groups?

If, in a particular school, in a particular county, in a particular state, the parents wish to open the school assembly with a prayer—whether the prayer be Christian, Jewish, or Moslem—why not? Let them alternate if there is sufficient interest. To continue to penalize a righteous activity under the stated freedom of worship doesn't make sense.

Furthermore, it's time we stopped appropriating large sums of money to enable those who don't like chaplains in the armed forces, "In God We Trust" on our currency, and appeals to Providence on the Great Seals of the several states to bring suit against the federal government for violating the First Amendment. We are a Christian nation, and when the citizens have a mind to change that situation, they have the ballot box to bring it about.

Just mentioned above are the Great Seals of the states. Here are a few of the classical Latin inscriptions by translation: "Under God," "God Enriches," "Nothing without Providence," "Under God, the People Rule," "The Life of the Land is Perpetuated in Righteousness," "He Who Triumphed Still Sustains," and "With God All Things Are Possible."

If I were a Jewish school teacher, I wouldn't want the Supreme Court of the United States to tell me that I should not wear my yarmulke when the student body assembles for three minutes of silent prayer because it violates the principle of separating the church from the state. And if I were an atheist teacher, I wouldn't want the principal of the school to compel my attendance at the God-worshiping morning assembly.

Awaiting you, the seniors, are the admissions offices of more than 2,000 colleges and universities. Supplementing these are nearly two hundred junior colleges and community schools. That, too, is pretty impressive, isn't it? Suddenly, however, we hear that our great public schools are in deep trouble. (You must have been reading about this in the newspapers and magazines.) Plagued by racial unrest, by the influx of illegal aliens, by a scarcity of well-trained teachers, by economic depression, by fears of nuclear disaster, by the crescendo of crime, and by the erosion of our moral standards, we desperately seek remedies.

Can our plight possibly be one of our own making? Is something being omitted from our school curriculum? Can it be that we have become so absorbed with our world materialism that we are abandoning the disciplined controls that the Founding Fathers wrote into our founding documents, minted upon our coins, engraved upon our currency, and required of all persons elected to public service or testifying in our courts the appeal of "So help me God!"

As private citizens or as servants of government—from the town meeting to the White House and the Supreme Court—are we abusing our freedoms while losing faith in our religious heritage? Must we anticipate cutting songs from the songbooks of 30,000,000 school children?

> Our Father's God, to Thee,
> Author of Liberty,
> To Thee we sing.
> Long may our land be bright
> With Freedom's holy light!
> Protect us by Thy might,
> Great God, our King!

Are we trying to make some kind of embarrassed apology to the authoritarian nations of the world for the inspiration that has provided—without respect to race, color, or creed—a refuge from both political and religious tyranny?

You should understand that this is not a course in general history. We cannot take time to cover again what you have already learned in your classes in American history. The emphases in this book will be quite different. Unless you are fully aware of the part that religion has played in the development of our nation, you will not be able to evaluate the effects of religion in other areas of the world. For reasons that are difficult to explain, we have not succeeded in making most American children cognizant of the source of inspiration that brought about the remarkable democracy in which we should be able to explain why America has always appropriately been referred to as a Christian nation.

Let us look at some comments taken from a marvelous book on the history of the United States.* It was published in 1965, the work of an internationally honored historian, Samuel Eliot Morison. Professor Morison reviews in a lively style, so different from most textbooks, the same events which are covered in all such histories.

> Elementary education—the three R's—became a parental responsibility by Act of the Bay Colony in 1642; and five years later settlements of fifty or more families were required to appoint a school master "to teach all such children as shall resort to him to write and read. . . ." The dynamic motive in colonial education

*Samuel Eliot Morison, *The Oxford History of the American People*, New York: Oxford University Press, 1965.

generally, until the rise of the high school and the state university, was religious as well as humane. Boys had to learn to read the Bible, to write and speak pieces in order to communicate; to cipher in order to do business. . . .

Some 130 alumni of the universities of Oxford, Cambridge, and Dublin migrated to New England before 1646. . . . Now that the English universities were closed to Puritans, the only way they could obtain a supply of learned ministers for their congregational churches and of educated men to carry on the work of civil government was to set up a college of their own. Without waiting for a wealthy benefactor, they went ahead and founded one through a grant of 400 pounds by the Assembly of the Bay Colony in 1636. Two years later the college opened at the new Cambridge in a small cow-yard given by the town. It was named after its earliest benefactor, the Reverend John Harvard, who, dying at the age of thirty, left to the college half of his fortune and a library of 400 books. . . .

The first printing press in the English colonies . . . was set up in 1639 in the Harvard College Yard, as the former village cow-yard is called to this day. Here were printed the *Bay Psalm Book*, the *New England Primer* . . . and the entire Bible in the Algonquin language for which the Reverend John Eliot of Roxbury devised the first equivalents in Roman letters. This was the first Bible to be printed in the New World. . . .

Almost all Englishmen of the seventeenth century were interested in religion, and everyone who read anything read works on divinity. . . . The Bible was well known and as thoroughly read in houses along Chesapeake Bay as on the Merrimack and the Connecticut River.

As you have learned, not all colonists were from England. The French, Dutch, and Spanish languages were heard from Quebec to Florida. The speakers were nearly all Christians by religious origin. Among the Protestants, sectarianism was rampant. The embattled Anglican Church, from which the colonists wished to be governmentally separated, was having to compete with Puritans, Methodists. Congregationists, Presbyterians, Quakers, et cetera.

Contests developed over boundary lines between the various land grants from European royalty to individuals and to groups. Sectarian laws were passed which opposed the participation in government positions of any who were not Christians. This was especially directed toward those who were Jewish immigrants.

Slowly the winnowing process went on until, contrary to all reasonable assumptions, the Continental Congress produced the Declaration of Independence. Military battles had been successful. The Confederation of States became the United States of America with a Constitution that guaranteed "certain inalienable rights" to all persons. The division of powers into executive, legislative, and judicial bodies became the marvel of the watching world. Man was not supreme. He remained the "sinner" against an infallible God through whose Son, the Nazarene, salvation and eternal life were to be assured. The new nation could be more accurately described as the end product of the Judeo-Christian heritage. The die was cast. The United States of America was a Christian nation. The government of the people, by the people, and for the people would attempt to live up to the standards set by the Bible.

With this much background, I would urge a bit of interesting personal research. Read the founding histories of the colleges and universities that you are considering for your continuing education. To help you, immediately hereafter is a chart listing the founding dates of 2,325 institutions from 1636 to 1980. All of these are functioning today! You will discover that between 1780 and the present, not a single year passed without the opening of one or more such institutions. Today, 481 of them still state their specific religious orientation.

Immediately following the first chart is a second one. It shows founding dates in relation to the growing population and immigration figures. This is a further statistical analysis of why America is properly referred to as a Christian nation—no matter how poorly we may, at times, perform under that banner!

When we have discussed those charts, we shall move on to consider some of the religions of the world in order to show that religion has been the universal experience of mankind, from the most primitive types to the most ceremonial and contemporary.

In studying these charts, pay particular attention to the notes and marginal suggestions that accompany the statistics. I believe you will not find this a boring assignment. For the first time, most of you will be looking at American history through the contributing factor of religion. This is the only intelligent way to study the history of any country or countries. World history is one, very long record of political frictions in which an inevitable element has been the religions of the contesting peoples. More often than not, it has been the chief element behind the motivation of warring nations.

All colleges, universities, junior colleges, community colleges operating in 1983, with their founding dates*

Year	Institution	Year	No.	Year	No.
1636	Harvard	‡1800	1	1837	11
1693	Wm. and Mary	1801	2	1838	7
1696	St. John's	1802	1	1839	9
1701	Yale	1803	1	1840	4
1740	Pennsylvania	1804	1	1841	3
1742	Moravian	1807	1	1842	11
1746	Princeton	1808	1	1843	4
1749	Wash. and Lee	1809	1	1844	6
1754	Colombia	1812	2	1845	7
1764	Brown	1813	1	1846	11
1766	Rutgers	1813	1	1847	11
1769	Dartmouth	1815	2	1848	6
1770	Charleston S.C.	1816	2	1849	9
1772	Salem, N.C.	1817	1	1850	10
1773	Dickinson	1818	2	1851	17
	Williams	1819	6	1852	12
1776	Hampden-Sydney	1820	1	1853	7
1780	Transylvania, Ky.	1821	4	1854	12
1781	Wash. and Jeff.	1822	2	1855	10
1782	Wash. Col., Md.	1823	2	1856	14
1784	Leicester J.C., Ma.	1824	5	1857	12
	Becker, J.C., Ma.	1825	2	1858	9
1785	Georgia	1826	5	1859	5
1787	Franklin and Marsh.	1827	3	1860	12
	Louisburg, N.C.	1828	2	1861	6
	Castleton, Vt.	1829	3	1862	3
	Pittsburgh	1830	3	1863	8
1789	Gerogetown	1831	6	1864	4
	Chapel Hill	1832	2	1865	18
	York, Pa.	1833	6	1866	16
1791	Vermont	1834	9	1867	25
1794	Bowdoin	1835	4	1868	11
	Tennessee	1836	5	1869	11
	Tusculum			1870	17
1795	Union			1871	14
1798	Louisville			1872	11

‡Note: from here on only numbers founded are given

*These institutions were available to the Founding Fathers, to their children, and to the colonists.

Year	Value		Year	Value		Year	Value
1873	15		1909	21		1945	10
1874	8		1910	12		1946	38
1875	11		1911	28		1947	30
1876	15		1912	15		1948	20
1877	7		1913	13		1949	15
1878	14		1914	7		1950	14
1879	9		1915	8		1951	5
1880	6		1916	13		1952	9
1881	19		1917	9		1953	10
1882	12		1918	14		1954	7
1883	17		1919	19		1955	15
1884	16		1920	13		1956	12
1885	22		1921	10		1957	24
1886	20		1922	16		1958	30
1887	20		1923	23		1959	11
1888	14		1924	14		1960	30
1889	28		1925	22		1961	30
1890	25		1926	23		1962	39
1891	30		1927	32		1963	49
1892	15		1928	16		1964	45
1893	17		1929	11		1965	92
1894	12		1930	12		1966	67
1895	16		1931	7		1967	61
1896	11		1932	12		1968	42
1897	13		1933	14		1969	31
1898	13		1934	10		1970	31
1899	18		1935	13		1971	17
1900	5		1936	7		1972	15
1901	17		1937	10		1973	10
1902	7		1938	7		1974	5
1903	14		1939	8		1975	2
1904	12		1940	6		1976	5
1905	10		1941	12		1977	3
1906	17		1942	7		1978	2
1907	12		1943	2			
1908	23		1944	4			

NOTE: Statistics on these charts are taken from *The World Almanac,* 1983, and the United States Office of Education.

The World Almanac for 1983 lists 2,325 colleges, universities, junior colleges, and community colleges—all above secondary level.

In studying U.S. history, it is very interesting to try to relate the ebb and flow of institutional foundings with:

1. Economics
2. Immigration
3. Warfare
4. Race problems
5. Popular unrest
6. Industry
7. Science
8. Religions

As a starting point for your research, consider an explanation for the years: 1957–70. Then you might try: 1918–1928, and 1881–1891.

	Ratio of population	to	Institutions of higher learning			10-year increase in population figures	10-year immigration figures
1790	3,929,214		29 =	1 to	135,490		
1800	5,308,483		37	"	143,472	1,379,269	
1810	7,239,881		45	"	160,886	1,931,398	
1820	9,638,453		63	"	152,991	2,398,572	8,385
1830	12,866,020		94	"	136,872	3,227,567	143,439
1840	17,069,450		157	"	108,722	4,203,430	599,125
1850	23,191,876		235	"	98,688	6,122,426	1,713,251
1860	31,443,321		345	"	91,140	8,251,445	2,598,214
1870	39,818,449		464	"	85,815	8,375,128	2,314,824
1880	50,155,783		574	"	87,379	10,337,334	2,812,191
1890	62,947,714		767	"	82,070	12,791,931	5,246,613
1900	75,994,595		917	"	82,973	13,046,881	3,687,564
1910	91,972,266		1,062	"	86,602	15,977,671	8,795,386
1920	105,710,620		1,201	"	88,018	13,738,354	5,735,811
1930	122,775,046		1,380	"	88,967	17,064,426	4,107,209
1940	131,669,275		1,474	"	89,327	8,894,229	528,431
1950	151,325,798		1,626	"	93,066	19,656,523	1,035,039
1960	179,323,175		1,779	"	100,799	27,997,377	2,515,479
1970	203,302,031		2,266	"	89,718	23,978,856	3,321,777
1980	226,504,825		2,325	"	98,139	23,202,794	3,962,475

Increase in population 222,575,611   49,125,213

since 1790   −49,125,213   22%

Native-born citizens 173,450,398

78%

Using the figures of the U.S. Immigration and Naturalization Service, we can establish roughly some interesting figures to support the claim that the United States is indeed a Christian nation:

Our population in 1820 is estimated at 9,638,453. Most of that figure—American Indians not counted—came from European countries, largely Christian (Protestant and Catholic).

The statistics show that between 1820 and 1979:

73.9% of immigrants from Europe—predominantly Christian.

19 % from the Americas, Australia, New Zealand—predominantly Christian.

92.9% predominantly Christian (Protestant and Catholic).

7.1% from the Middle East, India, Israel, and Southeast Asia (Islamic, Buddhist, Shinto, Hindu, Confucianists, Taoists, Parsi, Jewish).

(Note: the percentage of Christians in this latter group is too small to be significant.)

(Note: There are virtually no black people in the immigration figures. Those who came by slave importation have long since given up tribal religions and become Christians.)

Noteworthy, however, is the nature of the immigration pattern in the last 20 years:

1961–1970	1971–1979
85% predominantly Christian	62%
15% other religious backgrounds	38%

Increasingly we are becoming a multiracial, multireligious nation to whom our Christian government gives Christian welcome and freedoms that exist in few other places in the world.

It is this freedom which gives us not only the privilege but ALSO THE OBLIGATION TO LET OUR SCHOOL CHILDREN KNOW WHAT MAKES OUR NATION UNIQUE. HEREIN LIES NO VIOLATION OF THE FIRST AMENDMENT.

Together, in His Name

One hot, bright summer afternoon
I struck the bronze bell in a Buddhist temple,
But I was unmoved by the sound.
It should, I thought, have thrilled me
With it reverberating tone.

One clear, cold winter's night,
With moonlight etching shadows on the snow,
The priest intoned his ritual, his frosty breath
A cloud of white.

The tapers flickered on the altar
Before the dimly lighted gods.
He struck the great bronze bell,
And then I learned just how a temple bell
Should sound and what it means to have
Chills coursing through one's blood
As I observed anew man's everlasting
Quest for God.
I softly spoke a prayer
And sensed its union in the frosty air
With one the Buddhist monk intoned.
"Amen!" I whispered, knowing well
That God had heard that temple bell.

L. R.S. (1925)

Chapter II

Each to His Own

In our study of world religions, we can properly agree to the accuracy of three statements:

1. That religion serves to reconcile man with his environment;
2. Religion looks upon life experiences as being either *good* or *evil*; and
3. Religion encourages man to seek *good* rather than *evil*.

With that agreement, we turn to another demonstrable truth: the criteria for determining what is *good* and what is *evil* vary widely through time, cultures, and civilizations. In more cryptic language, "What is one man's meat is another man's poison." Surely we cannot be so naive as to expect agreement in the placing of items on the ledger of *good* and *evil*. Consider just a few of man's variations in thoughts and practices:

Human sacrifice	The urge to	Monogamy
Materialism	martyrdom	Warfare
Witchcraft	No future life	Spiritism
Hell and Heaven	Pacifism	Self-denial
Astrology	Miracles	Reincarnation
Plural marriage	Alms giving	Burnings at the stake

Turning the other cheek

Scarification of the human body

Love your enemy

The Devil

Sexual permissiveness

Thou shalt not kill

Guide me, O Thou Great Jehovah

An eye for an eye

I am the captain of my soul

Missionary motivation

A choir of Angels

All these can be found on both sides of the human ledger of things *good* and things *evil*. All are either supported or condemned within the religious communities of the world. Even so recently as 150 years ago, man's ability to communicate on a worldwide basis was notably limited. Religions functioned under geographic insulation and isolation. Today, representatives of these faiths sit side-by-side in the General Assembly of the United Nations; they face one another across a thousand conference tables in the capitals of the world.

This is history in the making! That is why your school believes that education has a responsibility to present contemporary religious facts as a portion of the foundation against which you will shortly be making critical judgments. Religion, more than any other single factor, has written world history of past ages. You should know that.

As we study eleven religions that embrace about two-thirds of the world's population, you will be amazed by the variety of practices that man has promoted in his efforts to communicate with a Supreme Being. They range from reliance upon the witches' brew in *Macbeth* to the mortal clad in gorgeous vestments as he elevates the Host in the Gothic cathedral; from the poisoned spear-tip seeking the tribal enemy to the penitent kneeling at the altar in tearful confession.

The universality of the spiritual compulsion in human beings is a fact that we now ignore in public education. We should be listening to the rhythmic beat of tribal feet on the continents of the world—in tropical rain forests, on burning deserts, and in the mountain vastnesses of the soaring Andes. Is there no message for us in the archaeological remains of ceramic animals, servants, and furniture destined for the comfort of the departed in a future existence?

Out of this complex of cultures have come man's codes of conduct—the mores and moral standards that we describe as being *either good or evil*. Furthermore, we ask, "Should this knowledge be reserved only for Christians—for Catholics and Protestants?" Surely it is owed to American children who are members of our Moslem, Jewish, Hindu, and Buddhist families. All are *our* school children.

Neither shall we fail to make an honest presentation of the enlarging voices of Humanism, the religion of self-worship based on the conviction that man is the apex of evolutionary processes.

Perhaps the introduction at this point of a true story would be relaxing as well as informative:

A senior class of American children in an independent school were halfway through a survey such as the one you are now beginning. In the class were representatives of the Islamic, Jewish, Christian, and oriental faiths. In simple terms, their colors were black, white, yellow, and shades of brown. They were asked to respond to the following assignment:

"Please submit questions to which you would like answers —questions asked in sincerity and without prejudiced arrogance. Base these upon what you have learned so far in this course."

Here are the questions which they submitted:

1. Do you own your own personal prayer rug?
2. All those statues in the niches and alcoves of your cathedral—why are they there and what do they mean to you?
3. Why do you bathe in the Ganges every morning? Isn't it terribly dirty?
4. The water which you just sprinkled on that baby's head—what did it do for the child?
5. Why do women cover their heads in your place of worship? In our church the men wear hats.
6. Tell me, why is that little bowl of rice placed before your ancestral tablet?
7. Just why are there always seven candles on the altar?
8. I am interested in the string of beads which you keep fingering. Why do you do that?
9. I am looking for the church with the flight of one hundred penitential steps. Where is it?
10. Do you mean that those two red eyes painted on the prow of your boat will keep you safe from shoals?
11. I hear that each of you places a gold ring about a finger of the other. Why?
12. You say that your ring is a wedding ring but that you have no husband. How is that?
13. The prayers that you repeat, minutes on end—why say them so many times? Doesn't God know our every wish without being told?
14. Do you mean that your religious founder was born of a great wave breaking in the golden sunlight on your sandy shores?

15. What good can come from sitting on that board filled with spikes? Are you trying to accomplish something special?

16. Did I understand you correctly?—the founder of your religion was born without human father?

17. What is that interesting necklace you are wearing? Don't those sharp claws bother you? What does it do for you?

18. What a task! To climb 2,000 steps on your hands and knees to the top of that sacred mountain! Wouldn't it be just as satisfactory to walk up?

19. You sit in meditation all day long. Why?

20. You always say your prayers while facing in a particular direction. Is there special merit in that?

21. That's very interesting—you tell me that the world will just go on and on, never ending, and that man will be either happy or miserable by the choices he makes. Do you really believe that?

22. Does everyone drink out of the same communion cup? Isn't that likely to spread disease?

23. If you sacrifice a goat instead of two doves, will you gain more merit?

24. What did you say when you knelt before that figure?

25. What is that little figure suspended from your rear-view mirror?

26. I notice that the priest rings bells periodically during the service. Why?

27. Why did you light the incense stick in that pot of sand before that terrifying figure?

28. Do you really believe that we shall burn in fire for eternity if we lead bad lives?

29. You say that the world will come to an end on January 14. Does it say so in your Scriptures?

30. Why did you just now light that taper in the little red cup?

31. You burn your corpses! Won't God need them when we arise at the Last Judgment?

32. Must everyone enter the temple barefoot? Doesn't that spread infection?

33. What a huge bell! You say the priest strikes it just at midnight. Why?

34. That tiny infant—just two minutes old—do you say he already carries the spirit of the spiritual leader who has just passed away?

35. Incense in the temple, incense in the synagogue, incense at the fertility dance! What's the purpose of a pleasant aroma as between man and God?

36. I hear that you may not have more than one wife. Is that true?

37. How many wives does your religion permit you to have?

38. Just look at that crowd of 25,000 people in yellow robes sitting in the square before that bronze figure! What are they accomplishing?

39. All those crutches, braces, and wheel chairs—do you mean to say that the people who came here using them have walked away without them?

40. That was a lovely story about looking for a lost lamb and not worrying about the other 99. Is this from your Scriptures?

41. Why does everyone have to make a pilgrimage to that particular city?

42. I understand that you must be married in a particular church under special circumstances if God is to approve the marriage. Do you really believe that?

43. You mean that he just laid his hands on them and they were healed?

44. What do you mean when you speak of "being washed in the blood of the lamb?"

45. Do you receive special merit if you put coins in that box?

46. Isn't one-tenth of your income a lot to give to the church?

47. You talk of secret and public prayer. What's the difference?

48. Do your people believe that all animals are sacred? The donkey that kicks? The bee that stings? The shark that attacks? The cobra that bites? These have the divine in them?

49. How can you "make a joyful noise unto the Lord" when you should "be silent and know that I am God?"

50. Your traffic is terrible. All those cars bringing 70,000 people to the stadium to hear a man talk about salvation!

Well, that's just a sampling of a much longer list of questions. If you know your family's religious faith, each one of you can probably find a question directed to you.

The preceding questions are directed to religions that are living in today's world. This is an appropriate time to talk about the "dead" religions. "Dead?" you may ask. Yes, indeed! Dead! Religions as fashioned by man seem subject to mortality even as is man. They come, they go, they die! What does *not* die, however, is man's everlasting quest for God, in whatever language He may be described.

If you will drop in at your school library for an hour's personal research, you can quickly assemble the gods of the dead religions. With many of these you are already familiar from mythological reading. Here are just a few:

Jupiter	Terminus	Baal
Diana	Dionysus	Apollo
Mithra	Jason	Thor
Chac	Osiris	Mars
Demeter	Hermes	Amon
Zeus	Hades	Aphrodite
Cybele	Isis	Artemis
Ra	Hera	
Itzamna	Athena	

Get from the school library a copy of Will Durant's *Life of Greece*, published in 1939. You will learn much!

From the Olympian heights above the blue waters of the Mediterranean, from the Fertile Crescent, and from the farthest flowing of the Nile arose paeans of praise. The creative arts thrived, and power mounted among the few. Enjoying assorted prosperities, man abandoned his fidelity in worship. Today we visit the magnificent ruins of the Parthenon, of the Roman Forum, of the temples of the Nile, and the overgrown altars of Tikal. Although the religions are gone, the warning voices of their prophets are still extant. Like the prophets of the Old Testament, they were without honor among their own people. The disciples of Jesus summoned people to repentance. Still later, Mohammad rebuked evil-doers. An echo of all those prophetic voices can be found in the lines of Oliver Goldsmith's "The Deserted Village":

> Ill fares the land, to hastening ills a prey,
> Where wealth accumulates and men decay!

Rudyard Kipling in "The Recessional" wrote:

> God of our fathers, known of old,
> Lord of our far-flung battle-line,
> Beneath whose awful hand we hold
> Dominion over palm and pine—
> Lord God of Hosts, be with us yet
> Lest we forget—lest we forget.

> The tumult and the shouting dies,
> The Captains and the Kings depart;
> Still stands Thine ancient sacrifice,
> An humble and a contrite heart.
> Lord God of Hosts, be with us yet
> Lest we forget—lest we forget!

Among the many voices we discover yet another, the poet Francis Thompson, speaking in "The Hound of Heaven" to whoever will listen:

> I fled Him down the nights and down the days;
> I fled Him down the arches of the years;
> I fled Him down the labyrinthine ways
> Of my own mind, and in the mist of tears
> I hid from Him.
>
> Still, with unhurrying chase
> And unperturbed pace,
> Deliberate speed, majestic instancy,
> Came on the following of Feet,
> And a Voice above their beat—
> 'Naught shelters thee who wilt not shelter Me'

Doubtless, there have been many religions of which we have no knowledge. Religions die, apparently, when they no longer serve the desires of the people. This can be stated in a more interesting way: When people find that religion gets in the way of a life-style that they are enjoying, the religion dies—not the life-style!

The secular Humanist—or as other titles might be applied: the Atheist, the Infidel, the Existentialist—has always been present in human society. These rebellions against the reality of God ebb and flow in human history. Whether among the Greek and Roman philosophers or the John Deweys of later date, they sparkle momentarily like the spring freshet that tumbles down the mountainside. They encourage a fragile blooming of man's reason, only to become the dried and rocky course from which no relief comes for man's thirst. Like the poor, they seem always to be with us.

The purpose of this study is not to stimulate assorted desires to proselytize among traditions other than our own. Ideally, all religious faiths should share in such a study of religion in human experience. A comparative study of religions is not a spiritual battleground whose end is to crown a victor! It is rather to learn how cultures and civilizations other than one's own have responded to the relentless pursuit of the Hound of Heaven. From such exposure, all mankind might discover a degree of tolerance unknown in this present world to which God has through the ages spoken in mysterious ways.

We need remind ourselves once more that such was the intent of our Founding Fathers when they made religion their first concern in the First Amendment to the Constitution of the United States of America. All people, of whatever faith or of no faith, are welcome to live in this land of freedom.

To examine more effectively the time-sequence of man's religious strivings, let us consider the chart on page 22.

The religions enumerated are part of the evidence that the human being is something rather special among the living creatures upon this earth. He is the only reasoning organism. All others act either intuitively and instinctively, or learn to conform by repetitive experience. Man thinks; man reflects. It is this *thinking, reflective* creature who has been and is responsible for the expansion of general knowledge and for the techniques of storing discoveries for the benefit of later generations. The medical sciences provide a simple illustration.

If I were to ask the pupils reading this book to name the physical senses, without much delay they would reply, "Why, seeing, hearing, touching, smelling, and tasting." Nearly all members of the animal kingdom have these sensitivities. We call them "common denominators." They are all physiological abilities. In the relatively short span of a few centuries, however, man has succeeded in analyzing the functioning of the human body to the edification of the television audience! We describe for young and old the wonders of blood circulation, the rhythms of the heart, the services provided by the intestines, the kidneys, and the liver. We diagram the networks of glands and nerves. Most recently we have displayed in full color "The Miracle of Life"—the intricacies of procreation from the conception to birth so that our growing children may comprehend how they came to be and how to care for the remarkable assets that have been given to us. We present this knowledge in our school textbooks and in our laboratories. All things we do rather well. We recognize with countless awards the achievements of the researchers.

Thus we come, belatedly I contend, to the all-important question: How do we justify the omission from our school curricula of *the only common denominator outside the field of the physiological*, namely the realm of the spiritual. It feeds upon the psychological subtleties of fear, anger, hatred, anxiety, mercy, justice, intolerance, compassion, love, and forgiveness. The universality of man's spiritual compulsion is as provable as is our acceptance of planets in our universe. Man has always been "on quest" for that which is greater than man—an identity to be feared, placated, appealed to for help, worshiped, and, in some fashion, ceremonialized. This study must also include with respect and tolerance that segment of human population, ever present, that regards man as highest in the order of beings in an evolutionary process. These adherents, too, are supportive of the thesis that man demands something to worship even though it be only himself. They also are religious by interpretation.

Now back to our Founding Fathers. It seems reasonable to conclude that they would not find in this study of world religions any attempt to fuse church and state, or to advance the cause of any particular creed to the disadvantage of others. The main objective is to help our multiracial, multireligious young people to understand the intimate relationship of the world's religions to history. We would urge children of whatever religious background to become more informed about the beliefs and practices of their own families. As we all do, so are we all seen to be.

Religions through the Centuries
Living Religions

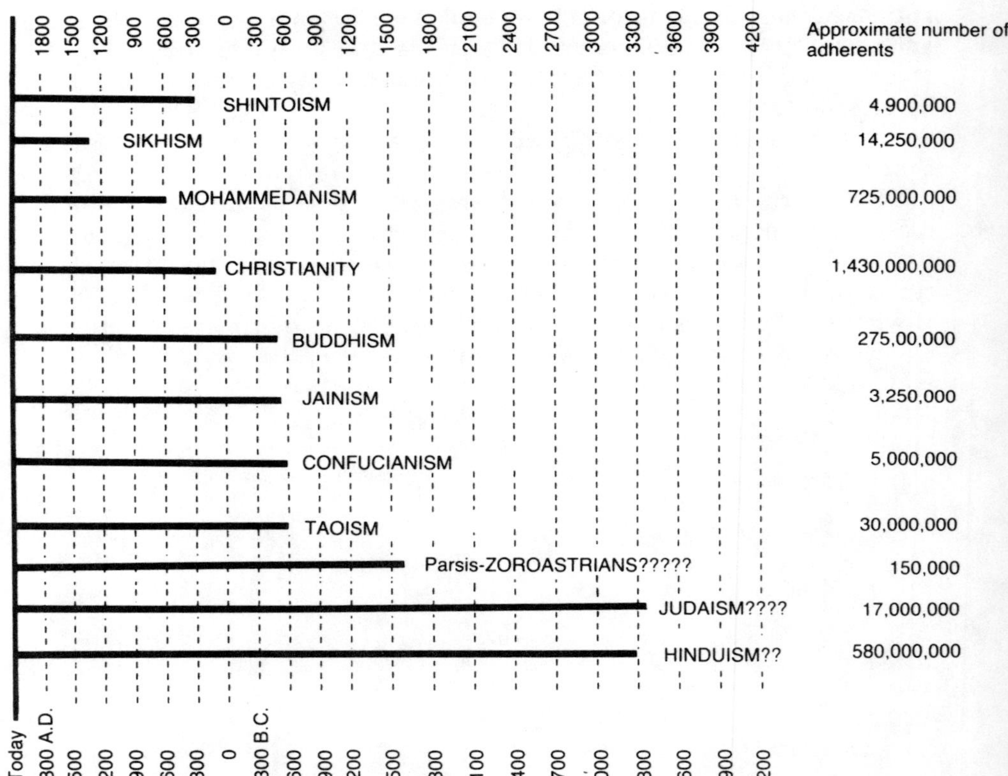

World population estimate 4,375,000,000
Religions above 3,085,000,000
Atheists, tribalists, spiritists
    etcetera   = 1,290,000,000

Chapter III

Who? What? Where? Why?

Your school library will inform you that there are more than 270 major languages spoken today on the continents of the world. With regional dialects, they number hundreds more. In every one of these languages you will find the equivalents of the question words above. Man is a creature of unlimited curiosity. He is forever asking questions and seeking answers. Now, I hope you will not be disappointed when I tell you that the ultimate answers to the questions above will not be found in this book—or in any other book for that matter.

When we but scan the volumes of research activities that crowd the library shelves, we conclude that man—the thinking, reflective creature—has always displayed a concern to be remembered by those who come after him. They will be asking the same questions. Centuries before written languages appeared, man was informing posterity by cave drawings that were pictorial descriptions of his activities and his beliefs. From kiln-baked impressions on tablets of clay and carvings in granite, we gather evidence of hunting. law-making, worshiping people. From the excavated entombments of the dead we learn—often in colors—of costumes, jewelry, and marriages. We learn of communication by water and by land and of conquests for territory.

Then came the written word, the result of experimentation by which the sounds of voice and environment could be preserved in symbols carved on wooden blocks. Paper and printing followed. Today these silent, phoneticized symbols reach the ears of the public by electronic impulses. At this very moment, we can receive and translate both sounds and images from man-made satellites millions of miles out in space. On one such traveling object are the outlined figures of two human beings—male and female—a message to yet undiscovered beings about ourselves. Who knows (to use one of the question words!)? Perhaps some creatures even now are listening to our disco music!

Words! Words! And more words! On monuments, on tombstones, in hymn books, in the Koran, in the Bhagavad-gita, the Analects of Confucius, the Buddhist Sutras, and the Bible! What an amazing compulsion to communicate with others not yet born! This very line that I am typing—how and when shall its message move mysteriously through time and space to stimulate a response in the mind of some high school senior whom I have never met? How have all these miraculous things come to pass? By a tremendous gaseous explosion in limitless space a billion or so years ago? Or does an omniscient intelligence, that towers over our tiny, finite minds, invite man to be on quest for that which is attainable by Faith rather than by scientific discovery? These are the alternatives that everlastingly pursue mankind.

Speaking of communicating, I cannot refrain from including an "education piece" that was prepared for adolescent sixth graders forty years ago. Education, some say, begins at birth! The selection really is closely related to what you have just been reading but directed to a much younger age-level. It may turn out to be more profound than you at first suspect. You will find that next in these expanding pages.

Words about Things about Words

The world is filled with countless THINGS
From "arrowheads" to tough "coil springs."
You make a "bench," or make a "box,"
An "aeroplane," or ticking "clocks."
A "kite" is "paper" on crossed "sticks";
A "house" a "pile" of well-spaced "bricks!"
And all these THINGS—from "tacks" to "shoes"
Someone has made for man to use.
   A bench provides a place to sit;
   A box becomes a camping kit;
A kite provides the young with pleasure
And ticking clocks help man to measure
How much time each new day brings
In which to go on making THINGS!

AND SO—
You see, a THING'S A THING!
You drop it, hear it, make it ring,
Or wrap it up to send away,
Or put it in some drawer to stay
Until ten years or so from now
You find it, and you wonder how
You failed to miss it up to now.

NOW the purpose of these lines thus far
Is just to point out that a star,
Adorned with milk-white nimbus ring,
Is still by grammar just a THING.
A THING of beauty, to be sure,
But only heaven's "furniture."

But then again it may be huge:
A laboratory centrifuge,
A hundred million bushel crop,
A cloud upon a mountain top,
Perhaps the mountain top itself.
(No item for your closet shelf!)

A THING may be a tiny bit
Of robin's egg shell, or a mitt
To snare the pitcher's toss to third,
Or just the whistle of a bird.
A THING is a word we use too much;
When we can't think of such-and-such!

WE KNOW—
There was a time long, long ago
When man's development was low,
Before he'd even learned to speak,
Or list the days within the week;
When everything from "rock" to "flame"
Had not the benefit of name.
THINGS could be felt, and seen, and heard
Just like that whistle of the bird
Appearing in line twenty-five,
But language had not come alive.

SO, many, many years went by:
The caveman heard his baby cry—
Repeated what his ears had heard
And "WOW!" became an early word!

By using sounds his voice could make
He named the fishes in the lake;
He found more words for "sticks" and "stones"—
For "moss," for "rain," for "flesh," and "bones."
And after quite a lengthy while
He had a most impressive file
To classify "boom!", "bang!", and "bing!"—
To say, in fact 'most anyTHING
That reached him through ear, eye, or touch—
Beyond those three, there isn't much!

Much later,

With a sharpened stick
He drew some pictures on a brick
Before he baked it in the fire.
Well, this just took him one step higher:
As, long before, he'd learned to fight,
He now discovered how to write.

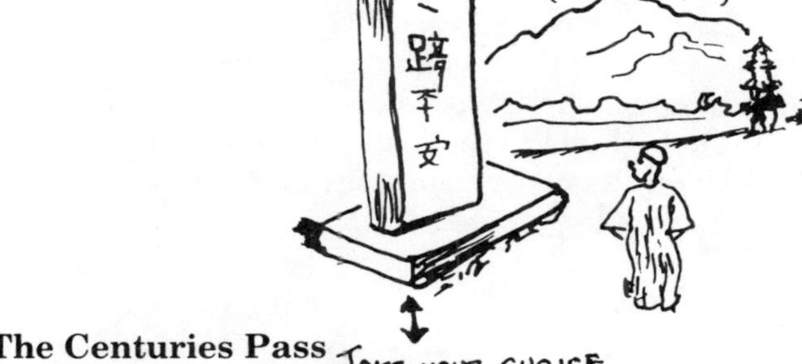

The Centuries Pass

The pictures change.
Calligraphy expands the range
Of items that a man could write
To join the list of "box," "bench," "kite"—
And then, an ALPHABET of twenty-six
With which to SPELL "stones," "bones," and "sticks!"

Of course, that gave a lot of pain
To boys who had to spell out RAIN, REIN, REIGN!
But Everyone from slaves to kings
Could now learn how to write down THINGS:
  a kite, a box, a bench, a cock,
  a boy, a girl, a bear, a rock,
the storm, the snow, the leaves that fall,
the sun that sheds its warmth on all.

But Man,
A creature of great pride
Was very much dissatisfied,
His language file was still too thin
To cover what had now crept in
To all his daily work and play.
He had to have new words to say
Just how he felt inside his heart
When tiger swallowtail would start
Its zigzag course across the field;
And when the golden eagle wheeled
In circles high without a stroke—
Then glided to the leafless oak
Upon the rocky mountaintop—
A most convenient place to stop!

That's why
Man had to have new words to say:
"delightful," "lovely," "joyful," "gay,"
"tremendous," "charming," "soft," and "loud,"
"impressive," "restless," "brave," and "proud."
These are the feelings Nature brings;
They are not ordinary THINGS—
Like benches, boxes, bears, and rocks,
Or aeroplanes and argyle sox!

So—
Just a dozen extra words
    To tell about the flight of birds,
Or how man felt about the
Spring
    That made his spirit wish to sing
Were not enough; for man had found
    That he was very closely bound
To other people just like him
    Who often tossed out *worth* for *whim*;
Who loved and fought; who shared and snarled,
    Who shoved and wrought, who cared and quarreled.
If he were going to live with them,
    He'd have to go to work again
To build a brand new list of words.
    (Not needed to describe the birds,
And not much good for naming "rocks,"
    Or "kites," or "bears," or ticking "clocks.")
They had to do with how man acts:
They recognized important facts
About the restless human being
Who had great difficulty seeing
That he'd have to think of *others*
As his sisters and his brothers.

Life would never be smooth sailing;
Man could not go swallow-tailing
Every day o'er meadows bright,
Resting after lazy flight.

Now Hear the words that joined the list—
(There is not one that may be missed!)
CONSIDERATE, POLITE, and FAIR,
And HELPFULNESS, and gentle CARE.
The parts of speech began to roll
From nouns like sturdy SELF-CONTROL,
Through adjectives: FINE, GOOD, and TRUE
To adverbs: BRAVELY, SWEETLY, too.
RELIABLE then joined the ranks
With GRATEFUL to express one's thanks;
CLEAN-MINDED, that's a hybrid word
But just as worthy to be heard
As HONESTY, FAITH, HOPE, and LOVE,
And REVERENCE for the GREAT ABOVE.
And as vocabulary grew,
Man could display how much he knew,
But also, to his own dismay,
How much he failed to do each day!

'Twas then man saw how much he'd grown,
As centuries of time had flown,
From THINGS like STONES and SAND and SOD
To great experiences like GOD,
WHO can't be seen, or touched, or heard
But WHO, just like the little bird
That whistled in line twenty-five,
Is surely very much ALIVE.

   Perhaps
We all can now agree
   That words were not designed to be
The basis for a spelling test,
   But rather to express the best
And noblest of man's thoughts and deeds.

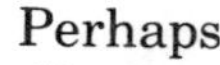

Chapter IV

A Letter and a Little Geography

Philadelphia, Pennsylvania
July 4, 1985

Dear Founding Fathers:

We should have been in touch with you long before now. Many of us have wanted to let you know of some of our present concerns, but we have been so occupied with racial problems, crime, immigration, and in particular the drug traffic, that we have postponed getting your good counsel. Independence Day seems the right time to write to you.

We enclose a copy of a little essay entitled "Words About Things About Words." As you will note, it closes with an appeal to our young people to show reverence toward God. The little sketches depict a church, a Bible and a Torah scroll. Do you think this violates your statement in the First Amendment to the Constitution with respect to the separation of Church and State? We feel that the little illustrated pamphlet expresses what you had in mind some time back. We suspect that we may not have done as well as you had expected of us.

We hope that you will be glad to hear of the course we are hoping to offer in "Religions and History." This is intended primarily for our clases in senior high school. We feel that we have an obligation to show our children, no matter what their religious backgrounds may be, that man has always looked to his religious beliefs for guidance in developing his codes of moral conduct. You people seem to have understood that better than we do today, five generations later. Or maybe it's because we've been allowing things to slip too much under that remarkable democracy that you folks set up in Independence Hall.

When our committee met last week, some of our members were reluctant to accept full blame for the things that are happening today. They recalled that your committees had some difficulties, too. It is recorded that some of you who fashioned the Declaration of Independence, which asserted man's inalienable rights, owned slaves. Those blacks, largely from Africa, were sold in public markets down South, you know, like cattle and swine. If not by you, then perhaps by some of your children and grandchildren who enjoyed life on their plantations.

Anyway, the situation got so out of hand that some preferred to break up the Union of States rather than surrender the slaves. In the conflict that followed—and we can't be certain just what news you had of it—over 200,000 men, many of them blood relatives of their adversaries, were killed. You had nothing to do with that, we know, but it must have been terribly upsetting when you learned of it.

Fortunately, our leader, Abraham Lincoln—a man both intuitive and pragmatic, delivered one of the greatest and shortest inspirational speeches in man's memory. . . . "that this nation, under God, shall have a new birth of freedom, and that government of the people, by the people, for the people shall not perish from the earth." Some of our school children today are encouraged to memorize the address. Other nations, with their benevolent or absolute monarchies, looked on incredulously as we put things back together again. That was a pretty close call, don't you agree?

While we were sitting around, chatting, someone got out a copy of General Washington's "Farewell Address." He reminded us that, while we were a God-fearing nation, we were also a nation "under law," and that the laws passed by Congress or at lower levels "were sacredly obligatory upon all until, or unless rescinded by procedures outlined in the Constitution." He said that should we forget that, we would be in deep trouble. Making laws was very serious business!

As we sat there reviewing our history, we concluded that we had done rather well, in a halting sort of way. We had become economically strong, our standard of living had greatly improved, and millions of unhappy people were pouring into our society from other countries. You may recall that that was when we got involved in a big international conflict, called World War I. We got into it a little late, but we helped to turn the tide against the Germans. Some of us were involved in that war. We don't often wear the medal we got for our participation. It honors us for sharing in "The Great War for Civilization."

Perhaps we became a little overrighteous when the war ended. A congressman named Volstead proposed that we ban nationally the sale of alcoholic beverages. The Women's Christian Temperance Union had a lot to do with its passage. President Woodrow Wilson didn't like the law and vetoed it, but Congress passed it over his head and it became law in January, 1919.

Well, that's when we got into trouble. We forgot about Washington's warning about the sacredness of law. From the highest to the lowest levels of our society we encouraged illegal smuggling and built up a friendly order of criminals! Wilson was right. We learned that we cannot legislate morality. It has to be cultivated by other channels.

Our apologies for writing such a long letter! We later went through a world-shaking economic disaster; we supported Franklin Delano Roosevelt's repeal of the Eighteenth Amendment, and got into another world war against Germany's Hitler and the Japanese. Again we entered late, but turned the attack on freedom.

Now you may find this hard to believe, but before the gun barrels had cooled, and before we could roll the fighter planes back into their hangars, we dashed off to Korea to protect the free people there from a new authoritarianism—the Communist forces of the People's Republic of China, an offshoot of the older Marxism of Moscow. We have never brought that Korean war to an end. Our armed forces still sit at the 38th parallel, with token help from the United Nations, maintaining the longest "cease-fire" in military history.

And you will have difficulty in believing this—shortly after Korea, we engaged in ten more years of struggle to defend the people of Vietnam from being taken over by communism. We failed in that. We are now virtually surrounded by the authoritarian governments who could not be less interested in governments under God. We make commemorative visits to our white-crossed graves at Anzio Beachhead, at Omaha and Utah Beaches, in Korea, and the South Pacific, bearing garlands and firing salutes. What have we done wrong? We need your advice, dear Founding Fathers!

We have not lost our desire for personal freedoms. We have, if anything, expanded them until legality and morality no longer walk hand-in-hand. Can we have lost sight of the concept of a nation under God? Repeated surveys still show that an overwhelming majority of the people still want to sing "God Bless America."

It's very late. We must get back to our families. As we leave, we stand to applaud the noble idea which you initiated so many years ago. We shall keep on trying!

Yours in admiration and affection,

C.R.O.F.I.G.
Committee to Restore Our Faith in God.

P.S.   We are asking postal authorities to forward this letter. We are not quite sure just where you are at the moment.

****

It is high time to return to our basic study. We are going to look at two unmarked maps of the world—no identification of continents, countries, cities, oceans, and rivers. Look at the first for a few moments. How confident do you feel about being able to pinpoint Sri Lanka, Tierra Del Fuego, Boston, Afghanistan, and Moscow? With the colored crayons of childhood, could you roughly fill in the area of South Africa, of the People's Republic of China, or the blue of Hudson's Bay water and ice? Even under the best of textbook teaching, history never seems to "come alive" unless we can visualize where history is being made.

This Mercator's Projection of the earth's surface is probably familiar to you from your earlier studies of the geography of our planet. Although the shapes of the land masses are somewhat distorted, think of this sheet of paper as being the total area of the globe. Of that total area, two-thirds are water surfaces; one-third is exposed land area. This globular home rotates on its axis every twenty-four hours. Beneath its green mountains, its prairies, deserts,and blue waters lies a molten mass of such intense heat that it explodes occasionally through the outer crust. A cooling process, begun long ago, is still in progress.

Many years ago, these land masses had drifted apart to form what we now see. Plants, animals, and man appeared. By a reproductive process, they multiplied before dying, thus assuring succeeding gen-

Map No. 1

erations. By "cross breeding," species developed subspecies. When you walked to school this morning, you admired the oak, maple, magnolia, or palm trees, depending upon where you live. You patted the Irish setter drinking from the fountain at your school entrance, admired the water lilies and the blue dragonfly hovering above. Overhead glided a vulture, or a frigate bird.

The book you hold, the pad on which you will write, the pencil in your hand—all have come from the forests of the world. The Stars and Stripes that you can see out the window came from the cotton fields of Alabama.

Just who are we? Where do we fit into that fascinating process of life development? Are we the end product of a long chain of reactions that is called "evolution," the linkage of which is still unclear? Or was man the unique creation by a supreme Intelligence—as something rather special who would gain mastery over the throbbing organisms and perpetuate his own likeness by the union of male and female, a procedure in force before man appeared?

For the second map, the assignment is different. The enchanting colored brochures of the travel bureaus—(see your Sunday edition)—have well educated you as to where pleasure is to be found on the broad sandy beaches of the world and how to get there with speed and economy. They are crowded with colored umbrellas and the relaxing figures of men, women and children. Can you mark these on the map? What you probably cannot do so readily is to mark those vast areas where human beings are disease-ridden and starving. Together with them, the unfortunate, we now number in excess of four billions of people. At present population growth rates, we can anticipate more than five billions in your lifetime.

Where did all this begin? Through the passing years, we have learned much from our men and women scientists, historians, and linquistic specialists. We can dissect the frog, name the night constellations, calculate the distance to Mars; we can count penguins in Antarctica on Monday and the migrating whales off Siberia on Thursday. We can estimate caloric and protein intake, and listen to *La Boheme* while jogging. As I write, I sit in air-conditioned comfort in subtropical Florida. Open before me lies a book with the pictured evidence of a tropical zone where glaciers once filled the valleys. On succeeding pages, I look, almost incredulously, at gigantic saurian skeletons from all over the world. Perhaps some of you will become paleontologists, or anthropologists, or archaeologists. Who knows? After all, we can't all become clerks, stevedores, dentists, lawyers, school teachers, farmers, and doctors! It's sad, but I cannot recall ever having made a single original

Map No. 2

discovery! I am grateful to the talented and the curious who have broadened my horizons!

Recently, I read in the news of a startling event. In clearing land for industrial development in Texas, the bulldozer uncovered the skeletal remains of a human being. Scientists, applying their techniques, set the moment of death some 10,000 years ago—about 8,000 B.C. The living person had been a woman about thirty years old. Death had come by a heavy blow on the skull. Who had she been? She could not possibly have known about the Great Wall of China, or about the Pyramids of Egypt. And most certainly she had never *read* anything like the Declaration of Independence!

We conclude, however, that she was not much different, in body and mind function, from the young women who today sit on the beaches under colored umbrellas, apply lotions, and hide immediate identity with dark glasses. We can assume that she had fallen in prehistoric love, had selected a mate, and had reared her children to respect the gods of the Aztecs or the Mayas. That we can know this much about her is attributable to scientific and historical research. We can be sure that, on every college and university campus listed earlier, the pursuit of truth goes on.

Mentioned above are those energetic scientists, historians, and linguists. We have applauded, and rightly so, their findings. Of the total world population, they comprise but a tiny segment. If we were able to query Winston Churchill, he would again say, "Never in history have so few done so much for so many."

I suppose we should not be surprised. Man has other more pressing concerns. Within the last fifty years, man has become fearful of and knowledgeable about the phenomenon of pollution—the fouling of our soils, our waters, and the air we breathe. *Dioxin* produces our own "deserted village"; our tax moneys refund the villagers' loss. Acid rain is destroying our forests. Oil spills annihilate the marine and vegetation life. We try to make sure that no cloud of insidious asbestos dust falls upon those who sit here reading about religions and history.

There is another pollution, however, that is far more threatening—moral pollution. It has been recognized for millenia. The Voice crying "Hear Ye! Hear Ye!" has been heard in all the languages in the world. The Voice is not the monopolistic experience of Christianity. It is the Ultimate Linguist warning against the erosion and abandonment of the indestructible constants of life that run like golden threads throughout all civilizations. They rise and fall as they are heeded or ignored.

What is wrong with American education? It has lost its spiritual focus. In our relative abundance and prosperity, we are discarding the time-proven restraints that gave direction to a God-centered nation. We were participants in the quest, but we have stopped looking. Somehow, and soon, teachers, parents, administrators, legislators, and governmental leaders must recapture the meaning of Lincoln's vision of "a NEW BIRTH of freedom." This has nothing to do with separation of Church and State. It is history in the making. We should be telling our children about it. What we need in our classrooms are teachers who believe in what the Founding Fathers so ably set forth.

God So Near

In early morning hour before the dawn,
When waning moon sails high
Above the chilly, blinking, starry sky
And floods its ghost-light on my window sill,
I am drawn to God.

Still later, when the gray of morning
Lights the east, and shapeless houses
Take on form against the slowly marching morn,
I wonder that, with beauty everywhere,
Mankind should cease
To worship God.

The pale, pale gray of dawn runs into pink.
The cool, cool stars of darkness fade away
Into the bright expanse of day,
And all the world waits breathless
On the very brink of God.

Sometimes, I think, we do not look for God at all;
Or, if we do, we seek so far
That He is passed by in the nearer view!

L.R.S.
1925

Chapter V

We Continue the Quest

We have raised many questions so far, haven't we? For many of them we shall probably find no final answers. Despite man's penchant for research with its resulting astonishing successes, the quest still continues among the peoples of the world for a better understanding of, and a closer relationship with, that which, in a multitude of languages, is best translated as GOD. Not that there is any shortage of answers! They have been legion.

This is a book about religions. Before we come to the last page, we shall have considered eleven of them. What more logical point can be found for beginning this review than the religious characteristics of primitive man? A common term now applied to these ancient people is "aboriginal"—the religions of the "aborigines." (Incidentally, those among you who may be so fortunate as to study Latin, might well improve your understanding by spending a few moments with your dictionary, discovering the origin and the meaning of such terms as *primus, primitive, primordial, primogenitor,* and *primogeniture.*)

Your *Webster's Collegiate Dictionary* describes the aborigines as the "earliest known inhabitants of a country." Where can we find these people? You will soon learn that they are no longer so "original" as they once were. So rapidly has man developed in the sciences that he now communicates worldwide in a matter of seconds. Exploration, wars of conquest, trade, industrialization, and the missionary efforts of the religionists—especially Christianity and Islam—quite naturally call to mind the words of the famous Negro spiritual, "There's no hidin' place down here!"

In your school library you will find many books and periodicals that will tell you where and how far you will have to travel to discover the last few pockets of primitive man's social and religious practices. You will find yourselves in the cloud-draped peaks and valleys of the high Andes, in the rain forests of the upper reaches of the Amazon, deep in the jungles in the tropical countries of Africa, lost in the shadowed valleys of the Himalayas, and crossing the hinterland of Australia. You will find them up the torrential muddy rivers of the islands of Indonesia where headhunters are still reported to dwell.

Perhaps we can best capture the idea of primitive man by indulging in the creation of a totally fictional setting of a contemporary history class in a high school just like yours. As you watch the characters develop, you may become, in your imagination, any one of them. You do not need to reveal which one you select; nor shall you have to write a paper on it as an assignment! The starting point for the journey we are about to take may be the town or city in which you presently attend school. That place may be, as dictated by circumstances, in Port Clinton, Ohio; or in Metuchen, New Jersey; or in Nome, Alaska; or in Dallas, Texas; or in Fresno, California. If you do not fancy those suggestions, you may choose a starting point that is uniquely your own. Let's be on our way!

****

The principal of Central High School—Mr. Peter A. Prober, M.A.—is chatting out in the corridor with Miss Fleurette Livingstone Michaelis Akbar. Peter's shining forehead melds gradually with the thinning hairs higher up and suggests eventual baldness. He smiles as he adjusts his half-lens glasses slightly lower on the bridge of his nose. Obviously he is enjoying this chance meeting with Miss Fleurette. Was it purely accidental? Well, we can't be sure, but that's another aspect of the story.

"Good morning, Miss Akbar!"

"Good morning to you, Mr. Prober," responded Fleurette.

"Tell me, Miss Akbar, what shall you be doing in your classes this week?" The nature of the question hinted at something rather unusual or special about Miss Akbar's classes.

"How good of you to ask, Mr. Prober! Most parents are still baffled by what goes on in my classes. Nothing quite like this has been found in our public schools of recent years."

Peter Prober, sufficiently diligent to have earned his master's degree at Columbia University, highlighted by a thesis entitled "Eth-

42

nological Adventures," had quickly taken in the flowered blouse, the beige jacket and skirt, the flawless texture of the Melaneselike face, the dark brown hair, and the sparkling black eyes. His interest in Miss Akbar was apparently genuine, but the reasons must remain speculative.

About fifty paces down the gleaming corridor is Room 204—Miss Aggie's room. The corridor's tiles are festooned with posters promoting attendance at the forthcoming high school dance. Already assembled in Room 204 in noisy banter are twenty-eight pupils—fourteen boys and fourteen girls. They are always on time for Miss Aggie's class. They are enrolled, with permission of the school's commissioners, in a study of the religions of the world. So far it has proved more interesting than calculus and a course in business economics! If we take just a moment while Peter Prober delays Miss Aggie's arrival, we may enjoy a quick look at the diversity apparent among the young men and young women who are waiting in Room 204.

First—a moving scene of hairstyles—blond and sprayed; black, straight, and glistening; short-cropped and kinky; dark brown and curly; teased and ballooned; stringy and neutral; reddish and tampered with; elevated or skull tight; roundly bunned or braided; combed or matted!

And those eyes—Nordic blue, Polynesian brown, African black, international gray-green; sparkling; sultry, fiery, brooding, and placid.

For clothing—evidently by common agreement—color-print dresses, or jeans for both sexes, topped by open-throat shirts of violent plaids.

As to stature—a wide range between 4′ 11″ and 6′ 7″.

Hands?—those that pass footballs, play the harp, finger the trumpet, shell peas, paint pictures, applaud country music, or apply Oil of Olay!

"But soft!" as Hamlet cautions, "Here comes Miss Aggie."

"Good morning, class!"

"Good morning, Miss Aggie!"

"I'm sorry I am a bit late for class. I was detained by talking with our principal, Mr. Prober. He is much intrigued by what we are taking up in class this year. I told him that we were beginning our study of primitive man. Where and when did he come into being? Did he have social characteristics that may be identified with what one finds today? Are there men, women, and children today who reveal similar traits and practices?"

An interruption—"Miss Aggie . . ."

"Yes, Abraham . . ." The class looked up with curiosity.

"Excuse, please, Miss Aggie. I have wanted to ask a question of you since the beginning of school, but I haven't had the courage until just now. Will it embarrass you?"

"Well, Abraham, how can I know before you ask the question? Please go on."

"It's about your name. I was looking at it in the school bulletin. I've never seen one quite like yours. I thought . . ."

The attention of the class was total! The long legs of the soccer and football players were withdrawn from the aisles. The nail polish that Grace and Tallulah were sharing was quickly slipped into a school bag.

"But, of course! It was thoughtless of me not to explain myself better when school opened. You see, I was born in New Guinea, a portion of the long Indonesian chain that you may have studied in your class in geography. My mother was French—hence the name Fleurette. My father was a Coptic Christian, born in Cairo, Egypt. He was a business man. His family name was Akbar.

"Now, my mother's mother—that is, my grandmother on my mother's side—do you follow me?—was married to an Irishman serving a professorship in the French university at Grenoble; his name was Michaelis Livingstone, an Anglican from Northern Ireland. So you see my mother was first a Miss Livingstone. She was born in New Guinea when Mike' Livingstone later shifted from Grenoble to a professorship there.

"Of course, both my grandmother and grandfather are now deceased, but my mother grew up there and subsequently married Mr. Akbar, the Coptic Christian business man, my father. So there you have the explanation of my name: Fleurette Michaelis Livingstone Akbar!"

"But how do you happen to be here in America—teaching this class?"

"Well, when I finished my early schooling under the nuns in a Catholic school in New Guinea, my parents sent me to the Sorbonne in Paris. There I spent two years. Then I was fortunate to receive a grant from an American foundation to continue my education in social anthropology at the University of Michigan. When I graduated, my application to teach in your school was successful, and here I am! My parents are still living in New Guinea in retirement. And here I am in this classroom! Although I was brought up in the Catholic faith, I now worship in the little Methodist church down near the Texaco station, since there is no Catholic church here. Miss Fleurette Akbar—but, evidently, better known as 'Miss Aggie.' There, now, Abraham, I hope that helps to clear up the confusion."

"Yes, thank you, Miss Aggie, but .. er . . . uh . . . You're sort of all mixed up, aren't you? What I mean is . . ."

"Oh, I see what's bothering you, Abraham. Let me ask you a question. Am I right in assuming that you are Jewish? That your parents may have come to the United States when Adolf Hitler was 'purifying the human race'? . . . Yes, I thought so. And probably inscribed in a lovely bound copy of the Torah are the names of all your family members for years back? Right? Just straight Jewish tradition as far as you have records. You're not all mixed up like me! I'm glad you asked your question. This little interruption may turn out to be very closely related to matters that we are going to discuss in our class in world religions.

"The questions that Abraham has just asked are very timely. This morning I am authorized by the commissioners to tell you about a most exciting development that concerns this class in 'religions and history' specifically. I have just told you that I was born and received my early education in New Guinea. Because of my interest in the subject that we are discussing, I entertained the hope of returning to Indonesia some day with a group of American school children. Our local merchants, through the leadership of our Better Business Association, have provided the funds necessary to send this class to Papua, New Guinea, during the two weeks of our Christmas vacation! Your parents have been informed and are willing that you should go. And our principal, Mr. Peter Prober, shall be going with us!"

[I won't attempt to describe the explosive effect that this announcement had upon the class. Throughout the football and soccer seasons, this astounding opportunity for the class in "Religions and History" was the main topic of corridor and "Hamburg Heaven" conversation. You seniors—the members of this class in whatever town or city you may have elected to reside—will be members of this high school expedition. For your information, the point of departure from the United States will be San Francisco, California.]

****

The skies were blue and the clouds white when Pan American's 747 soared out over the Pacific on a flight to Port Moresby, Papua, New Guinea, by way of Sydney, Australia, and the help of Qantas Airlines. It was late afternoon on December 22. They would be in New Guinea for Christmas. How strange it would be to see all the aboriginal people who inhabited the island!

As enthusiastic as the students was Peter Prober. He had promptly requested the school's librarian to make available from the periodical storage room some ten years of the bound copies of the *National Geo-*

45

graphic magazine, the *Smithsonian*, and *Natural History*. How he had pored over them when working for his master's degree in ethnology! All those photographs of assembled tribes people, dancing about the common fire pit! The glistening bodies shining under coatings of grease! The anklets and braclets! The bare-bosomed, dark skinned women holding babies in their arms! Here was the justification for the hours and the money he had spent in his pursuit of knowledge about developing mankind. And now it was his privilege to take young American school children to New Guinea!

To be expected were the whispered comments that the placing of their children under the chaperonage of Peter Prober, the unmarried principal, and Miss Fleurette, the delightful and good-looking teacher was but a further extension of the permissive society that increasingly won the applause of the young people and the more liberal elders. Although none of the uttered remarks made the newspapers, the community was aware of attitudes both critical and defensive among the sectarian denominations of the town's places of worship.

As the 747 circled for a landing in Sydney, Miss Fleurette's students saw nothing to suggest aboriginal people—towering hotels, broad paved streets, and, as they glided low for touchdown, rows of red brick dwellings suggestive of the old towns of England. Most prominent among all was the extraordinary opera house with its fragmented eggshell roofing, the very centerpiece in all pictures in the travel brochures. If there were any primitive bushmen in Australia, they most assuredly were not to be found in Sydney!

Accommodations in the new Holiday Inn reminded them of those they had just left in America. The trip to the famous zoological garden with its enclosed flyways was not like anything they had ever seen before. The giant suspension bridges spanning the waters of the harbor were filled with streams of traffic. Surely this was no land in which to look for primitive people!

"You see," said Peter Prober, "the Australian primitives are far from the populated areas—difficult of access—far to the west in the broad, undeveloped interior. Australia is now like America 200 years ago. They have the best of all modernities, and the ultimate settlement of the continent will probably be accomplished in far shorter time than was true for our country."

Qantas Airline took the party aboard the next day as they flew northward along and over the Great Barrier Reef, heading for Port Moresby in Papua, New Guinea. The young ones moved about constantly, sampling the views from the windows as well as the snacks the hostesses pressed upon them. The landing was smooth and the airport as up-to-date as those of other cities. Met by a travel agent, they were quickly driven to a hotel as modern as any at home. A huge swimming pool sat within the quadrangular enclosure of the gardens. Before the hotel lay the waters of the sea over which they had just flown. Under the shade of the casurina trees, "nannies" walked with the perambulators, caring for the children of the few westerners who still resided in Port Moresby as counselors to the newly independent government. Brown and olive-skinned young women, clad in color-print dresses, came from shop and office doorways, just the way young women did at home. No primitives here!

Early the next morning, December 24, they went by bus to the airport to board an Air Guinea flight to Mt. Hagen. They occupied 30 seats on the twin-propeller plane that seated about fifty people. Rising quickly, they flew over the cloud-covered ranges of mountains, patches of deep green appearing through the breaks in the clouds. It was not a long flight—just over one hour. Mt. Hagen is a mountain town with no acceptable transportation to other points by road. It stood high among the stretches of rain forest.

Suddenly, as they penetrated the cloud cover at about 12,000 feet, the plane banked sharply. Below lay a settlement—an extended clearing embraced by the surrounding forest. Obviously, this was no primitive village! Beneath the trees lining the streets appeared moving vehicles. The touchdown was smooth. Unsnapping their seatbelts, the young ones followed Peter and Fleurette as they descended the short roll-up steps. There at the foot stood their guide—tall, smiling, and good-looking.

"Welcome! Welcome!" called the handsome Papuan. "How good of you to come to see our country! They are waiting for you at the Golden Lily Motel. Come along! The bus is just beyond the customs barrier."

There followed much awkward handshaking, chatter, and laughter. With their packs on their backs, they piled into the bus, much as they would do at home every morning and afternoon on school days. Cautiously they examined their guide—their very friendly guide. They were looking for tattoo marks on his high cheekbones and yellow crescents on his forehead. There were no such markings. His jeans, like theirs, were marked "Taiwan," and the open collar of his button-down blue shirt read "Sears."

It was their principal, Peter Prober, who asked the first significant question. "Were you born here, Thomas?"

"Yes. Do you recall that pass through which you flew as you came in for a landing? Well, I was born in the valley the other side of that range."

"But your English is so perfect!"

"You embarrass me! I must credit the Australian teachers for whatever skill I have. That was after the defeat of the Japanese invaders. They sent my father to Sydney for legal training. We went as a family. Father is now a magistrate in Port Moresby. I am hoping to go to the University of Singapore this next year. Already I have passed their entrance examinations."

The run to the motel was not long, but the seniors had a chance to see the post office, a pharmacy, a hair-dressing parlor, and the headquarters of the YWCA. Primitive people? Where were they? Was Fleurette wrong in arranging for this return to her childhood days? Fleurette didn't seem to be worried. She was carrying on a conversation with Thomas in French. It appeared as a reunion of old friends. Peter Prober was occupying himself with his camera and new telephoto lens.

"Here we are," called Thomas, as the bus passed through a gateway and entered upon a circular driveway in front of the Golden Lily Motel. In the center of the flowered circle splashed a water fountain. They streamed out of the bus and into the lobby of the motel. Registration was quickly handled by Peter, who kept all their passports in his briefcase. The walk to their rooms took them past the bar where some half-dozen people were socializing. "Why, that's just like the motels at home!!"

All the boys were on one side of the long corridor, all the girls on the other. Peter and Fleurette had matching chaperone rooms at the upper end of the long series.

"Don't be too long settling in!" called Thomas. "Put on something light. It will be hot in the Sunday market."

"The Sunday market?"

"Yes, the Sunday market. It happens only on weekends. You will see hundreds of farmers with wives and children bringing their products for sale. They are also looking to see what they can buy or barter for at the many tables of merchandise. Some of these people walk for two days in order to get here."

"But do they know it's Christmas tomorrow? Will they come on the holiday?"

Thomas laughed. "To most of them Christmas means nothing at all. They have their own religious customs and practices back in the valleys. They are as much interested in seeing you as you are in watching them. They've seen many westerners since Australia first showed an interest in New Guinea, but perhaps not a whole group of school students like you. Come along, now. Be quick."

They were soon walking down the streets to the marketplace.

There was some delay when the girls insisted on buying postcards and stamps. Their families would like to hear about the aboriginals. Cards they found in a pharmacy serving soda drinks and even ice cream! Walking carefully to avoid the occasional truck and passenger car, they entered upon a huge open place crowded with human beings: hundreds of brown-skinned mountain people minding their piles of taro root, papayas, sugarcane stalks, and gourds. Basketry of intricate woven patterns hung from extended wires overhanging the tables. Gingerly, they stepped over the rock and pebbled footing of the marketplace.

Most puzzling of all the displays were the tables of brightly colored bolts of cloth that were stacked high on many of the tables. There was nothing primitive about the women who stood behind the tables encouraging buyers. Brown-faced and even black-faced, they cheerfully called to the passing crowd to make purchases.

Peter Prober was obviously both excited and perplexed. "Look, you kids. We can't all stick together. Thomas says it's okay for us to circulate among he crowd. We can't get lost. We can always come together down by that big pavilion where the cooked foods are being sold. He says that's like our American hamburg heavens!"

Three bown-skinned, happy-faced young women, obviously on the verge of maturity, stood listening to the appeals of the cloth seller. Their brightly tinted sarongs hung loosely from their slim hips. Their broad, bare feet seemed to be insensitive to the crushed stones over which they walked. They were laughing as they looked at the high school kids from America.

Thomas stood by with a look of amusement upon his face. Then he remarked in a low voice to Peter, "Look, coming here, a chieftain from the upper valley—see, the tall broad figure with the headdress of bird feathers?"

Peter was ecstatic. Turning to several of his party, he informed them of the approaching chieftain. "Get your cameras ready. Here comes a real aborigine."

The bulky figure strolled slowly, his bronzed body shining above the skirt of pandanus leaves that hung from a cord about his waist. His chain necklace of polished bird beaks scarcely moved with his steps. In one free hand, believe it or not, he carried a western umbrella, furled at the moment and revealing a purchase tag pendant from one of its ribs: "Made in Japan"!

It was Abraham, standing aside, who watched intently—not the passing chieftain—but Miss Fleurette. If she were "all mixed up" as his class question had suggested, she gave no indication of it now as she watched her students reacting to the scene. "Miss Aggie," he ventured, "You don't seem excited as we are. You just stand there and watch us! How come?"

"You forget, Abraham, that I grew up as a girl in West Guinea. Gatherings like these were common to my experience. Even then the impact of the modern world had touched the areas where I was reared. We did, however, get reports from the most daring of the explorers of interior tribes that lived a totally primitive life in so far as comparison with these you are watching today."

It was then that they had to move aside as a young black boy of about fifteen came through the tightly packed shoppers. To Abraham's astonishment, the lad was wearing earphones, and in his hands he carried a Walkman II radio. Obviously he was getting music from the radio station in Mt. Hagen, or perhaps even from so far as Port Moresby. Rather rudely, he pushed through between a blond-haired Anglican mother and the Chinese amah who was carrying a tow-headed child!

It was late in the afternoon when they returned to the Golden Lily Motel. They feasted on hamburgers and french-fried potatoes as they sat in folding chairs in the garden outside. Light from the moon and a circle of paper lanterns brought total relaxation. The rock music from the bar inside the entrance was subdued. Then, to their astonishment, new and different music caught their ears. Behind the hedge separating the motel from a small walled compound that opened onto another street came the faint chorus of voices: "Oh, little town of Bethlehem, how still we see thee lie. . . ." Yes, primitive man was disappearing. The questing for God, however, appeared to continue, even in this land of recent isolation from the rapidly changing world about it.

*   *   *   *   *   *   *   *

As for our school group, led by Miss Aggie and Peter Prober, why don't you bring them home by continuing the story? You could compose a collection of essays that would embrace the personalities of the class and the reactions of the community to their extraordinary journey.

Meanwhile there is further map work to be done. Immediately following is one now familiar in general outline. The purpose of the map's insertion at this point is explained in the textual material that accompanies it. Your copies of the *National Geographic* magazine will provide excellent source material. So will the countless travel circulars available in numerous agencies. Get to know your world and the people who inhabit it. This can become far more fascinating than watching the soap operas and the violence of drug warfare. It will increase your confidence that the association of religious and political history is essential in the educational curriculum of our public schools.

What has become of the primitive men, women, and children
of 500 years ago?

The dotted portions of the map indicate the areas where you *may just possibly* find surivors. Invaded by "more civilized" people who look for gold and ivory, or who seek to extend boundaries by conquest and war, they leave their happy valleys and, as refugees, cross rivers, climb mountains, and cross boundaries into strange countries. With them come their fetishes and idols. Before long, the carved god from Laos will hang side-by-side with the crucifix. New, synthetic religions appear. The totem stands beside the cross.

Go through your old issues of the *National Geographic* magazine. There you will find the disappearing aborigine.

Consult books in your library at school. Look up such words as ANIMISM, VOODOOISM, SPIRITISM, SHAMANISM. Your notebooks will soon be filled with gods and goddesses of which you have never before heard. They far outnumber those of the Greeks and the Romans. Abraham, Moses, David, Jesus, the apostles, and Mohammad will seem modern by comparison!

Why don't you make a class project out of this and pool your results as a school exhibit?

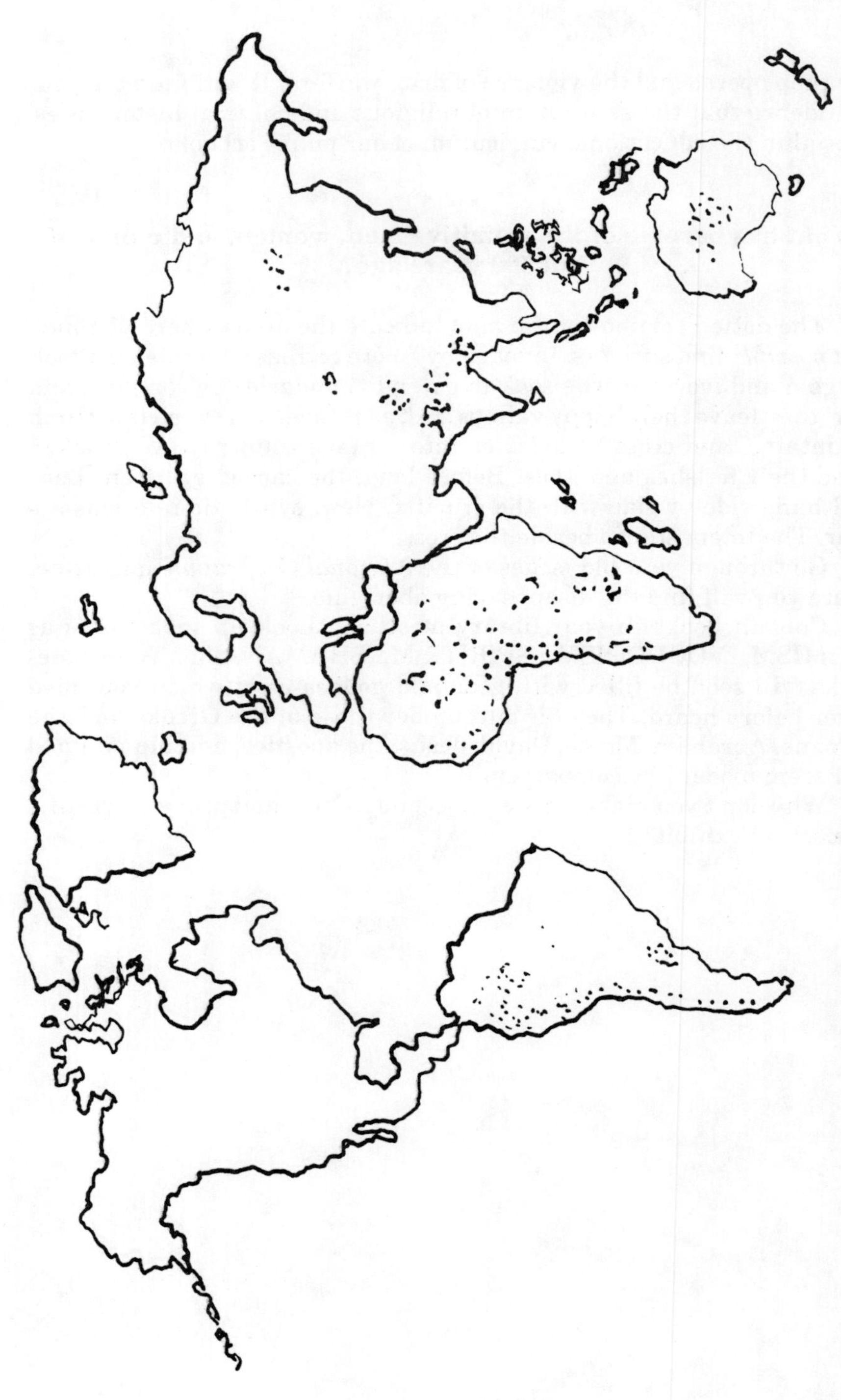

A Hundred Years from Now

Beneath these temple pines I sit
And dream of old philosophers
Who, too, have scanned these crumbling courts
And lifted up their reverent hands to Heaven.

And where I look with languorous eyes
Upon the dreamy, curving roofs
That lead my gaze in childlike joy
Up to the vagrant clouds, they too
Have looked.

A hundred years from now, perhaps,
Beneath these same white pines will sit
Another soul. And as he sees
These curving eaves, these age-worn courts,
Who knows?

He too may feel that Good is here,
That Beauty lasts from age to age;
Perhaps he'll even draw his brush
And write a simple little verse
Like this.

L.R.S.
1920

Chapter VI

From Fantasy Back to Reality

Amusing as it would be to follow Miss Aggie and her class back to their hometown, we must return from fantasy to reality. Our objective is to become more aware of the world's major religions. In this little book, however, there can be no in-depth study of the theological variations among so many different cultures. We shall accept the fact that a vast majority of the world's population—now numbering more than four billion human beings—do think about, call upon, fear, adore, and/or worship some power which, although unseen, outranks mere man in his worldly strivings.

You will discover that religion and politics do not walk along together like bosom friends, holding hands and smiling as they contemplate the happy life before them. The sectarian nature of both religion and politics provides many situations of interreaction, often approaching violence even within the boundaries of a single nation. To restate what you have heard before, there can be no intelligible study of history that excludes a simultaneous study of man's religions.

From your earlier attention to geography and history, you should have gained a good grasp of the appearance of the land areas of the world. We shall now take another look at those land areas in relation to the distribution of some of the world's major religions. We shall do this in convenient sections. You will find hereinafter three maps of North America, Central America, and South America. Listed thereon are the numbers of Christians, Moslems, Jews, Hindus, Buddhists, and others who are to be considered when undertaking a study of this type.

<h1 style="text-align:center">Central America (Middle America)
and the Island States of the West Indies.</h1>

The Bahamas and islands of the Greater and Lesser Antilles: Jamaica, Haiti, Dom. Rep., Puerto Rico, Guadeloupe, Martinique, Barbados, Grenada, Trinidad, et cetera.

Central America

Belize
Costa Rica
El Salvador
Guatemala
Honduras
Nicaragua
Panama

The figures given below are the combined count for all of them:

Christians	42,181,000
Moslems	151,000
Jews	11,720
Buddhists	86,300
Hindus	11,200
Atheists	919,000
Others	5,538,000
Total Population	48,898,000

See religious
population figures
on next page.

Religious Adherents on the North American Continent
Based on Population Estimates of 1980

Canada

Christians	=	22,364,000
Jews	=	337,000
Moslems	=	155,000
Hindus	=	45,000
Buddhists	=	18,500
Sikhs	=	8,000
Atheists	=	369,000
Others	=	1,279,000

U.S.A.

Christians	=	197,344,000
Jews	=	7,259,000
Moslems	=	1,883,000
Hindus	=	500,000
Buddhists	=	180,000
Atheists	=	400,000
Others	=	16,567,000

Mexico

Christians	=	67,866,900
Jews	=	48,600
Moslems	=	20,900
Buddhists	=	23,000
Atheists	=	40,000
Others	=	1,965,600

Summary

Christians	=	287,574,900
Jews	=	7,644,600
Moslems	=	2,058,900
Hindus	=	545,000
Buddhiss	=	221,500
Sikhs	=	8,000
Atheists	=	809,000
Others	=	19,811,600

318,673,500

NOTE: "Others" refers to many cults, spiritists, tribalists, folk religions, and small numbers of Parsi, Taoists, Confucianists, et cetera.

From your courses in history, you have already learned that the continents of the so-named "Western World" were populated with numerous Indian tribes long before the arrival of the European explorers and settlers. These new invaders were of both Catholic and Protestant background. Although there is some evidence that some of the North American Indians were evangelized, the relationship was really one of continuous conflict as the colonists moved west. These remnants of the North American Indian tribes now reside in reservations spread from coast to coast. From your reading and your watching of television, you are aware of what happened to the smaller units of unorganized tribal groupings. They could not prevail over the weaponry of the colonists.

South America

South America too, is predominantly Christian. The thirteen countries represented here cannot be given detailed religion listing for want of space. Instead, you find the combined listing of the thirteen countries whose major religions fall within our studies.

Notable among the figures is the large number of religionists who are classified as "Others." This is not surprising, since large areas of South America still reveal large numbers of the original Indian populations who had developed their own worship traditions prior to the arrival of the Spanish and Portuguese explorers.

In the vast tropical forests of the Amazon basin and in the almost inaccessible ranges of the Cordilleran mountains are still to be found religious practices that approach what modern man describes as "primitive." The arrival of Christianity resulted in a merging of primitive practices with those of the invading religions. Christian evangelism in South America remained largely the monopoly of the Roman Catholic Church from the fifteenth century until Protestantism moved in in the nineteenth century.

Central America, including the island settlements, and South America present a picture quite different from the conquest of North America. The land-sighting of Christopher Columbus in 1492—a date familiar to all American school children—was the opening wedge which, to use contemporary terms, initiated a super navigational freeway across the Atlantic Ocean. To create a metaphor, it was as though someone had shot a cultural arrow, largely Latin in craftsmanship, hoping that it might land in India! Instead, it fell among the Indian tribes of the western hemisphere.

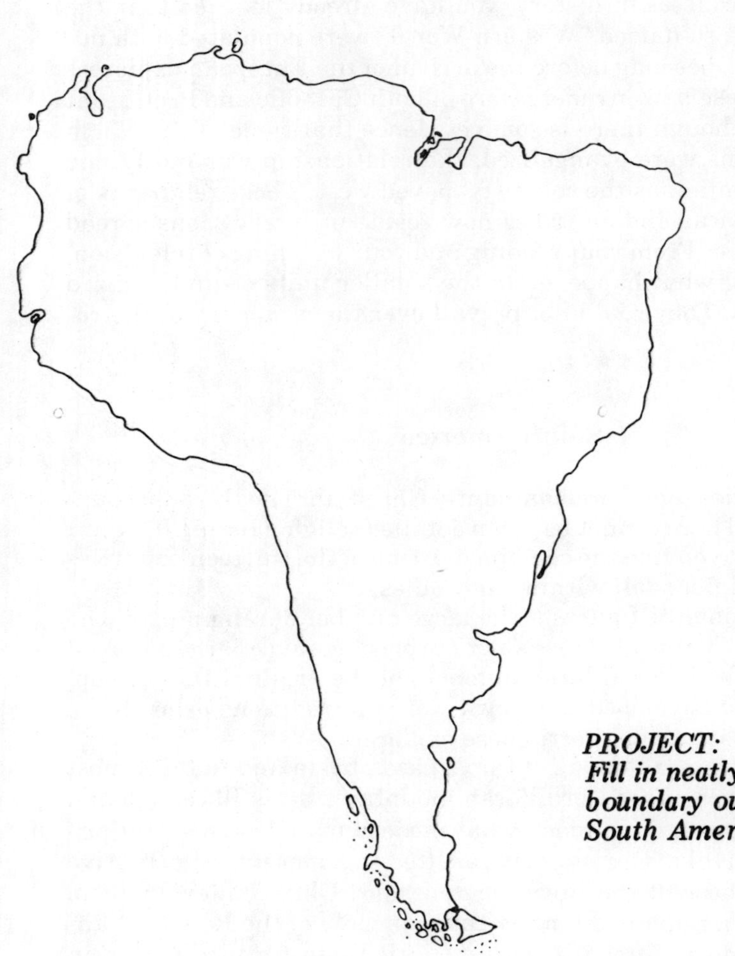

PROJECT:
Fill in neatly the
boundary outlines of the
South American countries.

Christians	235,489,110
Moslems	339,150
Jews	70,300
Buddhists	29,700
Hindus	314,150
Atheists	1,677,380
Others	11,064,180
Population =	248,984,000

The ancient Indian civilizations of the Mayas, Aztecs, and Incas, amazingly advanced in a variety of skills, had deteriorated prior to the arrival of the Europeans. The causes of this disintegration are still being sought by today's anthropologists, paleontologists, and archaeologists. Thousands of tourists annually trek southward to view the architectural remains of a most remarkable people.

It was with the remains of that cultural collapse that the arriving Europeans made contact. Once the metaphoric arrow had landed, the aftereffects spread north and south. The British, the French, and the Dutch followed the Spaniards and the Portuguese. Within three hundred years (1492–1792), "Europe" had captured the American continents. The resident native populations had been subdued and subjugated. The invading Europeans contended among themselves for territorial sovereignty over the vast lands that fell into their hands. Extraordinary military and negotiating activities took place as sovereignty shifted from one country to another, and as the Europeans continued to pour into the new world.

By 1792, the United States of America had come into being. In conjunction with the other European settlements, the United States became a party to the development of the African slave trade,which, before it was brought to an end in the middle of the nineteenth century, had peopled the agricultural fields of countless plantations from Virginia to Brazil with more than ten millions of marketable human property—free labor composed of enslaved human beings.

You young people who sit in our high school classes have covered earlier, and in more detail I hope, this tightly compacted summary. You are contemporary witnesses to the continuing efforts of this and other governments in the western world to grapple with the sociological problems that have emerged and expanded since the "freeway" across the Atlantic Ocean was unofficially opened in 1492! Indeed, the continents of the western world have been realistically described as a gigantic melting pot into which have been poured the ingredients of Caucasion, Black, and Indian cultures. The kettle is still being stirred!

We are now ready to assemble the 1980 figures on population by religions of these huge land areas.

	N. America	C. America	S. America	Totals
Christians	287,574,900	42,181,000	235,489,110	565,245,010
Moslems	2,058,900	151,000	339,150	2,549,040
Jews	7,644,600	11,720	70,300	7,226,620
Hindus	545,000	11,200	314,150	870,350
Buddhists	221,000	86,300	29,700	337,000
Atheists	809,000	919,000	1,677,380	3,405,380

| Others | 19,811,000 | 5,538,000 | 11,064,180 | 36,413,780 |

Total Population 616,547,190

Christians = 91.7%	Others = 5.9%	Jews = 1.3%
Moslems = .4%	Hindus = .14%	Atheists = .6%
		Buddhists = .055%

Now that we can accept as fact the dominance of the Christian religion throughout the Americas, your curiosity may have been aroused by the presence of more than two million Moslems and considerable numbers of Hindus and Buddhists. All of these people are very far from the world areas where their religions were founded. Both Hinduism and Buddhism long predate Christianity. How do these people come to be in such numbers in the western world?

In reality, their presence is not a mystery. The reasons for their being so far from "home" are well known. Why not make out of these known facts a research project for the class? Among the many reasons offered for the recent decline in the quality of our public education is one that is too seldom brought to our attention: the failure of our classroom teachers to make real to their students the excitement of personal discovery. Far too many of our classroom teachers have not themselves had the experience. Both teaching and learning have degenerated to the reading and memorizing of textbook material, the administering of true-false tests, and the subsequent dismal grade-graphs for discussion at the next meeting of the faculty.

Please do not misunderstand me—there is nothing wrong with reading, memorizing, and responding to tests. This formula has been in effect for several thousand years in all literate world cultures. The stumbling block is rote memorization. This class could quite easily memorize the masthead of the Congressional Record in one session of the class. One week later it would have vanished beyond recall. The best memorization is unplanned and subconsciously propagated by one's becoming involved in some act of personal discovery. The challenge of research is a technique for mind training that can be initiated as early in a child's life as there is intellectual response. Never mind how fully exploited a given field may be by others who have gone before. Don't worry about the repetitive nature of the results. To the growing mind, the field is new. Only from minds so set on fire come the original discoveries that later change the course of human events.

Now then—why don't you try to find out why there are so many Hindus in Guyana—more than 300,000 of them? You will find the research quite fascinating.

Chapter VII

A Further Look at Europe

Although the conquest of the Americas by Europeans partially occupied their attentions for several hundred years, we note also the outward thrust in other directions during the same period of time. Improved geographical knowledge and navigation skills also sent them scurrying southward and eastward at this time. With the Portuguese taking the initiative, other European nations soon skirted the African continent and made their way to the remotest points in the vast Asian land mass. Although there had long been overland trails connecting the west with the east, sea exploration greatly facilitated the speed of the movement. Of this movement we shall learn more when we take up the study of Far Eastern religions; for the moment we should fix our minds upon one general statement: the cultural outthrust of any homogeneous civilization, whenever it may occur in historical time, explodes like skyrockets and rains showers of creative illumination upon the surrounding cultures. If you are interested, you can read endlessly about the rockets that were sent up by the Chinese, the East Indians, the Moslem world, the Egyptians, the Greeks, and the Romans.

While so reading, you would also note that these periods of creativity and illumination have been accompanied by political conflicts, aggressive seizure of territory, military action, economic distress, and eventually cultural decline. We should have this in mind at this time when Europe was sending up its rockets—the three hundred years from 1492 to 1792.

This three-hundred–year assault upon the Americas, Africa, and the Far East by Europeans was not made by cultural illiterates. For 1500 years Europe had been the cultural beneficiary of the Greeks, the Romans, the Egyptians, and the Far East. The magnificent architectural achievements, the scientific discoveries, and the mathematical skills of the "ancients" had far outdistanced the "barbarians" of Europe. Capitalizing upon what had been learned, the Europeans had now graced their lands with impressive cathedrals of Gothic and Romanesque style, with libraries of hand-written, color-illustrated books, and with observatories for the scanning of the heavens. Even late-coming Islam had made its contributions.

What Europe was now contemplating was the expansion of trade and commerce—not a burning desire of the religious to carry the Gospel of Christ to the whole world. Europe had its collective eye, to use a modern term, on the "bottom line," the dollar, or shall we say upon the pound-sterling, the guilder, the franc, the lira, the mark, and the peso?

Well, you might ask, weren't those European countries engaged in trade before 1492? Yes, indeed! Christian Europe had been interested in the Middle East and the North African coastal countries for centuries. But good business always seeks to become better business! The invasion of barbaric Europe by the Romans had been followed by the emergence of Christianity through the sacrificial efforts of the disciples of Jesus. By the fifth and sixth centuries, places of Christian worship were spread throughout England and the mainland of the European continent.

What we are hoping to do in this classroom is to set the stage for the first, well-recorded conflict between two of the world's greatest religions—Christianity and Islam. For more than six hundred years after the death of Jesus, Christianity, despite the persecutions it underwent at the hands of the Romans, became the dominant religion of Europe and much of the Mediterranean area. At first subservient to Roman law, it finally conquered Roman paganism and, through the established church, took over political control. Kings, queens, princes, and a variety of monarchs "took on the Faith." In general terms, one can say that Christianity had subdued politically the tribal religions of what history has called barbaric Europe. To create another metaphor, we might say that the Christian skyrocket that had soared heavenward to greet the star of Bethelehem had now illumined Europe.

Then suddenly, as the cinema scripts would describe the incident, a once inconspicuous and unremarkable caravan-trade attendant, learned in the trails that led from Saudi Arabia to the borders of India, began visionary experience with the monotheistic God of the Jewish people. Mohammed (570–632) listened in his many trances to the ONE GOD of all people. Mecca thus became the historical starting point of a great religious leader and his enthusiastic followers. Out of his visions came the *Koran*, the bible of the Islamic people. It was to be the final revelation of God's will to the last of the prophets, the judgment of Islam.

The new religion spread with incredible speed throughout the Middle East and along the northern coastline of Africa until it reached the Atlantic Ocean. Both Islam and Christianity now held a joint interest in the city of Jerusalem. Meanwhile, Islam had also crossed from North Africa into Spain and France. The long drawn-out struggle between the Christians and their Bible and the Moslems with their Koran included the two centuries of battle over the city of Jerusalem—the Crusades, A.D. 1095–1291.

The stage is now set for the confrontation—the religion of "love" was to be challenged by the religion of the "sword." The contest is still in progress in 1986!

****

Class Projects

You are aware by now that this textbook is not a detailed, full-fleshed history of religions. Rather, it hopes to be an "instigator" to research at the high school level. This is an appropriate moment to make some simple suggestions. Absolutely essential to the teaching program of any school is the availability of a library of books, periodicals, and volumes of general reference. Staffed by trained and imaginative librarians, it invites the classroom specialists in mathematics, the sciences, languages, literature, and history to share in interdisciplinary projects.

Mathematics becomes involved with world population and disease epidemics. Science moves from the study of the elements to the exploration of space. Languages become absorbed with communication, people to people. Literature moves from the boring mastery of grammar and rhetorical techniques to the creative urge to poetry and prose. History passes from a mere chronological sequence of dates to man's everlasting struggle to obtain some degree of equality in the distribution of food and the other perquisites of life among the world communities of human beings.

Creative, imaginative teachers, alert to interdisciplinary cooperation with their colleagues, can make the learning experience of the students an exciting adventure. The customary practice of assigning "a composition of your own choosing" will then, and only then, provide an incentive to eager minds.

The topics to be chosen are limitless. Why not select one or more of the following topics for your own research paper?

1. The Ships of the Age of Exploration
2. The Canadian Buddhists
3. Agricultural Crops of the American Indians
4. The North American Rivers as Aids to Conquest
5. Primitive Medicines
6. Languages and Dialects
7. A History of Land Grants to Immigrants
8. Human Slavery as a Worldwide Phenomenon
9. The Practice of Sacrifice in Religious History
10. Birds and Animals as Reported by Explorers
11. The Marriage Customs of American Indians
12. Books, the End Product of Exploration

Develop your skills at keeping orderly, systematic notes of all your reading. Don't let your notebooks become a meaningless jumble of your friends' telephone numbers, the shopping list for the stop at the supermarket on the way home from school, or a convenient place to practice your aspirations to become a cartoonist! Whereas the illustration below may suggest some lighter moments and the relaxed

mind—it now makes more sense for us to return to our major project. On succeeding pages are more maps. They are accompanied by comments that will help to clarify your minds with respect to what we are attempting to accomplish. Be of good cheer! This may turn out to be more mind-stimulating than you had expected!

To comprehend the significance of the world's religions in the shaping of world history is no little assignment. We have had a brief look at the primitive, aboriginal man. We have learned that he is rapidly disappearing from the face of the earth.

We've discovered that truly primitive people are indeed hard to find. And we are aware that out in the Far East are more religions that we have just barely mentioned. We'll get to them later.

Christianity and Islam

What we are about to consider, however, are the adherents of *Christianity and Mohammedanism, who will be vying for the allegiance of the total world population in the years that lie ahead.* This map limits itself to the initial advance of Christianity before the arrival of Mohammed. Faithful to their teacher Jesus, proclaimed Son of God, the original disciples and those who came later carried the news of ultimate salvation throughout the Middle East and then onward through the Mediterranean area. There was no implication of military power in their message. Indeed, they were cruelly persecuted throughout the lands of the Greeks and Romans. Their minds and hearts were attuned to a "Love," the quality of which had never before been brought to the ears of man. They were not interested in conquest, in the overthrow of governments, or acquirement of wealth. Their conquest was that of man's heart and spirit.

See what they had achieved by the time that Mohammedanism came into operation—A.D. 622.

By A.D. 600, the Christian message had been carried, by sea and by land, to all the areas here marked with the Cross.

Four of the apostles suffered martyrdom: Stephen, Paul, Peter, and Mark. The Good News had reached all parts of Europe, including England and Ireland, and the Scandinavian countries.

Despite Nero's persecution, there were some 3,000 Christians in Rome in A.D. 57. Pope Clement announced in A.D. 94 that all of the Roman Empire had been "Christianized."

Of course, the quality of belief was diluted when mass conversions were called for. Scattered all over this area were thousands of Jews unpersuaded by the teaching of the disciples. Their persecution and slaughter in Spain and elsewhere would match the heinous crimes of Adolf Hitler.

The Christian Imperative—

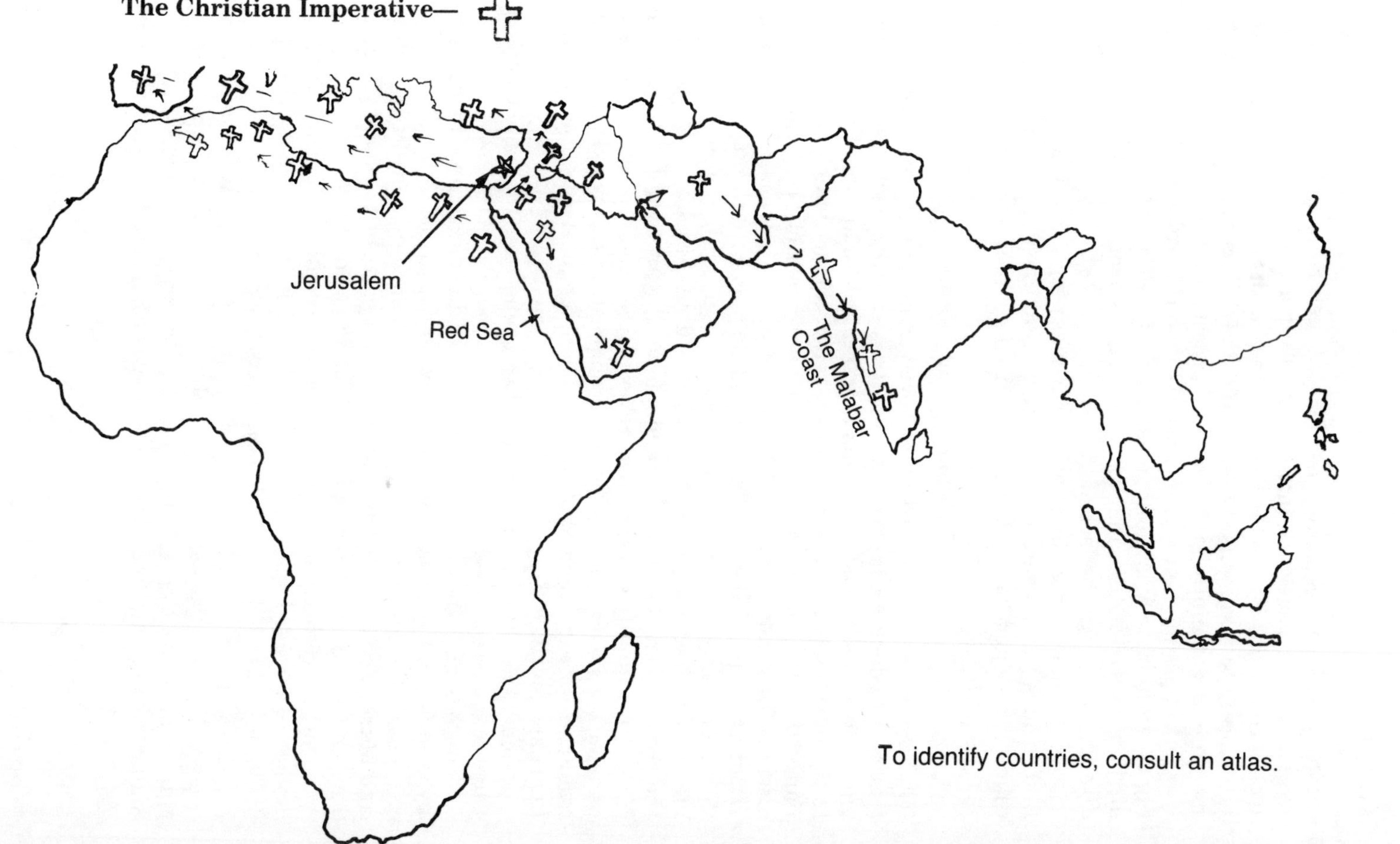

The bottom line is that "Christianized Europe" was ready to take over the Crusades (1095–1291), and to colonize in Africa AND the Americas in the "AGE of EXPLORATION." ISLAM, too, will be in motion!

Accepting the Old Testament acount of the origin of the world, of the prophets, and the prophetic status of Jesus, we note the arrival on stage, by Islamic claim, the final prophet by God's ordainment —Mohammed. He is the final authority. All truth is recorded in the Koran—the revelations taken down by his relatives and close friends during periods of trance.

Following public discovery in A.D. 616 of ideas that suggested his autocratic aims, his fellow Meccans of the great Arabian peninsula oppose him. Mohammed retreats, is besieged in Medina, negotiates, escapes assassination, cleverly outwits all opponents, and clearly wins domination of the Arab peoples. From the beginning, his protection was armed force. Attacks on caravans to provide economic relief; a battle with the Meccans convinced the onlookers of his prowess (A.D. 624), and the next year (A.D. 625) he announced that all the people of the Arabian Peninsula who did not recognize him within four months, would be subjected to force. This was followed by messages to all known sovereigns and rulers that he would assure them of safety if they would embrace Islam. He had the use of artillery to accompany his armies. When he died, he was making plans for the conquest of Syria.

Syria fell in 638 and Egypt in 641. Within 200 years, Islam had taken over most of North Africa and the Middle East. Islam reached the southern coasts of Europe and established settlements in Spain and France. *Most of the Christian penetration of Africa and the Middle East was destroyed by the military might of Mohammed's faithful followers.* These successes would be challenged in the crusades for the recovery of Jerusalem (1095–1291).

For over three hundred years, Islam had India in its control under a succession of dynasties. Their course was steadily eastward and northwestward until Islam claimed adherents among the peoples of the southeast Asian islands and among the Chinese of Mongolia and the area of Peking (1200–1500).

The cultures of all these regions were influenced by Mohammedanism, especially in their remarkable architectural creations. Visitors to today's India will find startling contrasts between the architectural abilities of Islam and those of the Hindus.

The age of exploration would find Islam and Christianity face-to-face in expanding their areas of religious influence. Both religions would find increasing sectarianism within their own adherents.

The Islamic Imperative—

Beginning with the death of Mohammed in A.D. 632

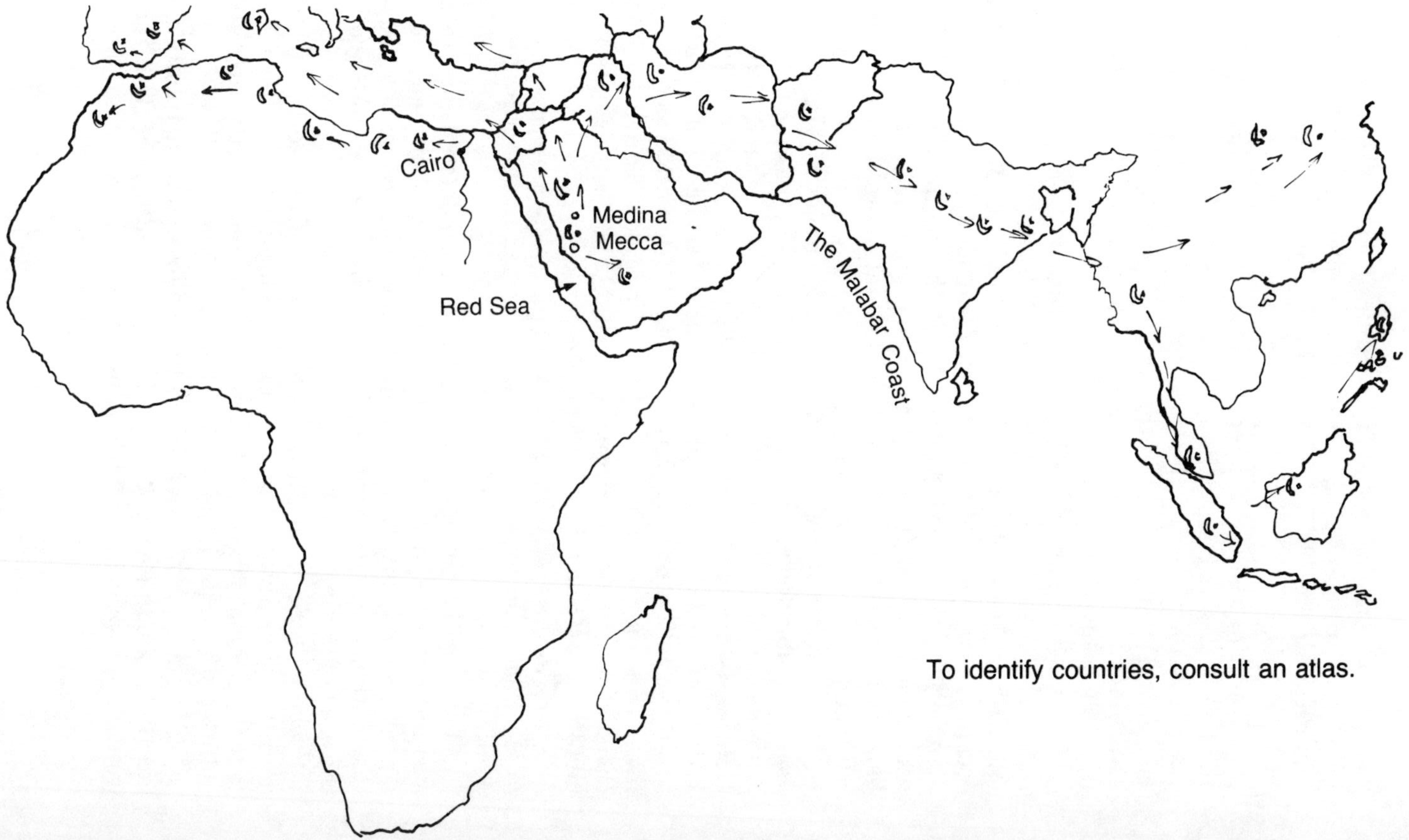

To identify countries, consult an atlas.

Yes, I know! You are becoming restless for some information about those other religions that have been mentioned—the Hindus, the Buddhists, the Shintoists, the Parsis, the Sikhs, the Taoists, the Jains, and the Confucianists. Please be patient. Before moving to those ancient faiths, we ought to fix firmly in mind the trio of contemporary religions that are so immediately related to the political events that are reported almost hourly on radio and television in our homes, schools, and businesses: JUDAISM, MOHAMMEDANISM, and CHRISTIANITY.

From these three faiths have emerged virtually all the elements of political confict in the Americas, Europe, and the Near and Middle East. These three religions, despite theological differences among themselves, comprise a religious trinity that steadfastly opposes the Marxist atheist, authoritarian minority that is in our time encircling, with notable success, hundreds of millions of human beings—religionists of many faiths—with the announced intention of destroying all religious beliefs. Numerically, these Marxists are but a tiny fraction of the world's population.

Their successful expansion, beginning most obviously with the Russian revolution of 1917, has been based largely upon two factors: 1. the failure of the religiously oriented countries to solve the problems of poverty and other social inequities, and 2. the amassing of military equipment by the Marxists of such volume as to give reasonable assurance of their success in carrying out their purposes.

This triumphant expansion can best be illustrated by listing the countries of religious orientation which have fallen under the political control of communism.

Afghanistan	China	Hungary	Mongolia
Albania	Congo	Kampuchea	Mozambique
Angola	Cuba	Laos	North Korea
Benin	Czechoslovakia	Latvia	Poland
Bulgaria	East Germany	Lithuania	Romania
	South Yeman	Vietnam	Yugoslavia

Paralleling the spread of the controlling Marxist philosophy is another demonstrable fact: More than twenty governments now sitting in the United Nations assembly are military juntas or "military governments" that have taken over from previous forms of government. Behind each takeover lie conditions of social distress or corruption. To what extent have governmental failures in the religiously oriented countries been responsible for this upheaval in human society? That's something for us to be thinking about as we examine the Jewish-Moslem-Christian opposition to the "godless society."

Judaism

To begin, several things should be pointed out as significant when considering the Jewish people: 1. They are credited with originating the concept of monotheism—that God is the Creator of the Universe, and that God exercises spiritual authority over all the peoples of the world; 2. Both Christianity and Mohammedanism had their roots in Judaism's monotheism; and 3. The Jewish faith, unlike Mohammedanism and Christianity, was not, and never has been, a "missionary religion" seeking converts to the faith. Generally speaking, one is born into the Jewish faith.

The origins of the Jewish faith go back in time some 2,500 years B.C. As you may have gathered from the chart of the world's religions earlier in this book, Jewish origins virtually preceded Buddha, Confucius, and Lao Tze. The drama of the development of the first Jewish nation was played out on a portion of the world map that can be illustrated by the two rectangles herewith.

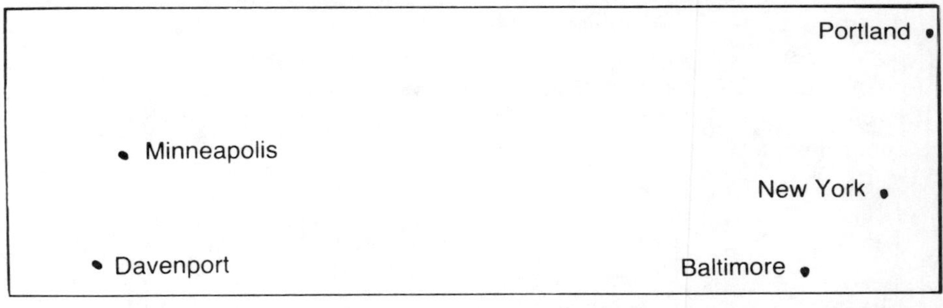

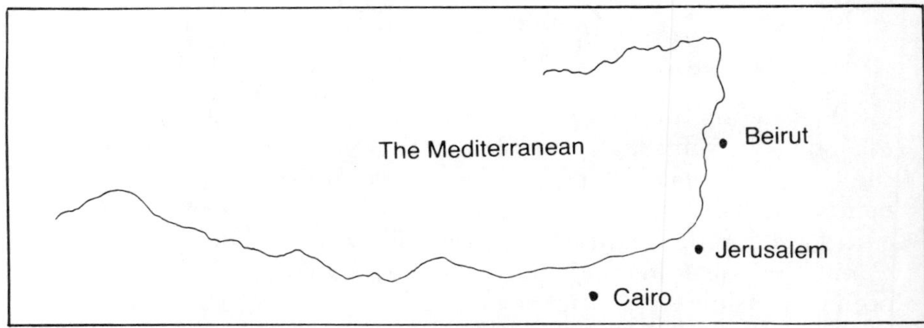

The scales are identical

72

Here you see again the necessity of combining the study of religions and history with world geography. In broad, general terms, the entire history of Judaism (4,500 years), has been staged in an area comparable to an American rectangle embracing such points as Baltimore, Davenport, Iowa, Minneapolis, and Portland, Maine. With the cooperation of the airlines, you could today have breakfast in Baltimore, lunch in Davenport, tea in Minneapolis, dinner in New York, and go back to bed in Baltimore! The same journey on the comparable map would have lasted for more than a year with travel by cart, camel, and sailing ship!

To telescope Jewish history into this limited space is hazardous and almost inexcusable. We do require, however, a framework of reference before we move on in our discussion of religions and history. Our most easily available source of recorded history is the Old Testament of the Judeo-Christian Bible. In particular we should read the first five books, known as the *Pentateuch* and ascribed to the authorship of that monumental figure, Moses. I would venture the statement that although the Torah and/or the Holy Bible can be found today in most homes of the two religious traditions, not one individual in a hundred, of either persuasion, has read either out of curiosity or in association with worship Genesis, Exodus, Leviticus, Numbers, and Deuteronomy.

By such negligence we are missing the foundational structure of both Judaism and Christianity. The so-called "soap operas" that today claim the daily attention of millions on modern television are dwarfed by the story of Abraham as laid out in detail in the book of Genesis. That stalwart Semitic tribesman developed a covenantal relationship with his monotheistic God that would eventually be passed on to both Islam and Christianity.

Looking for excitement in your reading choice? Genesis has it all: murder, adultery, warfare, bribery, incest, deceit, violence, family fights, and marital infidelity. The time of the setting was about 2000 –1800 B.C.

We accompany the nomadic tribal group under the leadership of Abraham as they move out of Ur of Chaldea toward better pastureage "up north." It was really Terah, Abraham's father, who had the urge to move. They were living in somewhat austere lands east of Cairo, Egypt, in what we know as Arabia. He would stop competing with others and depart with a rather select group, inviting his son, Abraham, and wife, Sarah, along with Abraham's first cousin, Lot. So a relatively restricted caravan of men, women, children, camels, sheep, and slave attendants got under way. Furthermore, Terah was getting old. He was well on his way to 200 years.

Well, they must have made pretty good time, considering the means of transportation and eventually reached a settlement that went by the name of Haran. If you're looking for it on a Bible map, that was up near the Turkish border. There Terah died at age 205 years. Abraham, at the youthful age of 75 years, now had the responsibility for carrying on God's mission. Their instructions from God were to head south with their flocks and their slave labor. They were thus moving into Canaan. God had already told Abraham that he intended to make out of Abraham's people a great nation. Appreciative of this special attention, Abraham erected an appropriate sacrificial altar.

Unfortunately, just at that time, a famine fell upon the land. The logical move under such circumstances was to continue south to Egypt in Africa where the ever-faithful Nile River provided abundance. As they approached Egypt, Abraham revealed to his wife, Sarah, a private concern. Sarah was reportedly a most beautiful woman. Some Egyptian, he feared, might not hesitate to kill Abraham and take his wife unto himself. Sarah consented to be introduced as Abraham's sister to avoid such a possible happening. And that is what was done upon arrival in Egypt.

What a mistake that was! King Pharaoh promptly snatched the lovely Sarah for his harem! Abraham must have been horribly embarrassed and frustrated when the king's assistants brought him many gifts at the behest of King Pharaoh.

Inevitably, Pharaoh discovered the truth. Here we can do wisely to quote directly from the *Living Bible.**

From Genesis 12:17–20: But the Lord sent a terrible plague on Pharaoh's household on account of her being there. Then Pharaoh called Abraham before him and accused him sharply. "What is this you have done to me?" he demanded. "Why didn't you tell me that she was your wife? Why were you willing to let me marry her, saying that she was your sister? Here, take her and be gone!" And Pharaoh sent them out of the country under armed escort—Abraham, his wife, and all his household and possessions.

What you have just read is but a tiny fragment of a remarkable recording of a very sensitive and durable people. Now you can follow on your own the developing fortunes of Abraham's descendants—often the offspring of a concubinage system so widely practised throughout the world before the restrictive influences of Christianity appeared.

Beautiful Sarah died at 127 years of age, having borne Isaac to

---

*Published by Tyndale House, Wheaton, Illinois, in 1971. By November of 1973 there had been 37 printings totaling more than 16,000,000 copies.

Abraham in her old age. Abraham married again and fathered many more sons and daughters to keep Isaac company. Death came upon him at age 175.

Meanwhile, son Isaac had, at forty, married a very lovely girl from Syria. Her name was Rebekah. Abraham was adamant that, in marriage, Isaac should not become attached to one of the Cananite girls and had sent emissaries to locate an acceptable maiden. Rebekah's willing return began one of the most repeated love stories of the Bible. When she gave birth to twins, Jacob and Esau, she and Isaac really launched a series of events by which the scripts of "Dallas," "Dynasty," "Guiding Light," and "General Hospital" appear as simple as "Peter Rabbit" or "Goldilocks"!

We shall now accept the passage of about 600 years (1800 B.C.) when you can continue the story by reading Moses's autobiographical narration of how he led the enslaved Jews out of Egypt. For forty years they would wander through unfriendly and inhospitable lands and peoples, having passed through the parted waters of the Red Sea. Of course, if you have seen that oft-repeated classic of *The Ten Commandments*, starring Charlton Heston, your pleasure in reading will be much increased. We can be confident that Moses at the time had not the slightest suspicion of the anguish that all those "shalt-nots" would visit upon people for generations to come!

Sad to say, Moses never made it into Canaan, the land of "milk and honey." His people, however, under Joshua, Moses's number-one assistant, did manage the takeover. It didn't happen suddenly. Even before Moses died, there had been some pretty clever intelligence collecting by advance groups. It's something like reading the activities of the more modern CIA!

With the final assault, however, there was much blood shed before the establishment of the Chosen People could be proclaimed.

Then began the much-heralded kingdom of a united people. The first king was named Saul. Saul was succeeded by David, a genius for organization. He was also a pretty fair poet. (When you get home from school today, pick up a copy of the Bible and turn to the *Twenty-third Psalm*.) Son Solomon succeeded his father, David. He, too, was an able young man who also wrote poetry and lyrics. In point of fact, the years of the House of David are still regarded by Jewish people as "The Golden Age."

When Solomon died, however, things took a turn for the worse. His son, Rehoboam, brought about a division among the people into two kingdoms, the Northern and the Southern. He chose to run the Northern Kingdom, which they named Israel. The revered name of

Judah stayed with the Southern Kingdom. Public opinion thereafter always maintained that the Southern Kingdom was the better of the two. They were probably right.

In 722 B.C., Rehoboam's state was overrun by the Syrians, and that was that! Judah held on until 386 B.C. From then on, the beleaguered Jewish people were subjugate to the Persians, the Babylonians, the Greeks, and the Romans. You have already been over that period in your classes in ancient history, I'm sure.

The final blow came when the Romans, in A.D. 70, please mind the date, destroyed Jerusalem and along with it the TABERNACLE (THE TEMPLE), the very center of JEWISH RELIGIOUS COMMITMENT. The tribal structure that was traceable to Abraham collapsed; the Jews dispersed all over the world. The anticipated coming of the Messiah who would redeem the nation had not taken place. They rejected the claim for such a Messiah by the Jewish disciples of a new figure who had appeared upon the scene—Jesus, the Nazarene, who claimed to be the Son of God.

The location of the Jewish tribes is still a matter of research. Anthropologists have long tried to identify those tribal elements without success.

This is the right time to present the figures that reveal where the Jewish people may be found today. The chart which follows is based upon the statistics assembled and published in *The World Christian Encyclopedia*, Oxford University Press, 1983.

Once again, in the long framework of charting events both religious and political, the children of Abraham, Isaac, Jacob, and Moses are today tying together the threads of 4,500 years of history. The theater for the restaging of this monumental drama is the identical building in which Isaac sat in the producer's box to watch the histrionic skills of his father, Abraham. The proscenium arch remains about three hundred miles wide, although it has obviously been repaired countless times. The frayed curtains still open and close to the confusion of the bewildered audience. Upstage, hanging at a precarious angle against the wall, is an ancient clay tablet bearing the engraved title of "The Ten Commandments."

On the battered stage are still many of the original properties—sheep, camels, green oases, and Bedouins. Missing are the Canaanites, the Amorites, the Jebusites, the Hittites, and the Philistines. They have been replaced by the Lebanese, the Jordanians, the Syrians, the homeless Palestinians, the Druse, the Iranian terrorists, and most recently by some Italians, French, British, and Americans. Watching from the box seats are the Russians, the Saudi Arabians, and the Egyptians.

No longer do camel caravans, laden with tents, move through the time-worn cobbled streets. They have been replaced with armored tanks and personnel carriers. Overhead the gunships and the fighter planes have usurped the territory of the storks, the swans, and the eagles.

Unchanged within the enormous cast, the Israelis parry, thrust, and retreat. Watching intently from the balcony are Moses, David, Solomon, Elijah, Jeremiah, John the Baptist, Peter, Paul, Caesar, and Mohammed. Surely we should arrange for our high school students to have complimentary tickets to this colossal production. Word has already been spread abroad that some of them have already slipped into the balcony seats with Herod, Pontius Pilate, and the good Samaritan!

World Distribution of Jews—1985

United States	7,259,000
Israel	3,847,000
USSR	3,120,000
France	598,000
Argentina	540,000
Un. King. and Ireland	466,000
Canada	337,000
Brazil	206,000
South Africa	158,000
Romania	104,000
Hungary	94,000
Australia	75,000
Uraguay	58,000
Iran	54,000
Mexico	49,000
Belgium	42,000
Ethiopia	34,000
West Germany	32,000
Netherlands	32,000
Switzerland	22,000
Sweden	16,000
Morocco	15,000
Columbia	14,000
India	11,000
Chile	10,000

<table>
<tr><td>Colombia</td><td align="right">13,700</td></tr>
<tr><td>Spain</td><td align="right">9,300</td></tr>
<tr><td>Austria</td><td align="right">9,000</td></tr>
<tr><td>Tunisia</td><td align="right">9,000</td></tr>
<tr><td>Yugoslavia</td><td align="right">8,000</td></tr>
<tr><td>Zimbabwe</td><td align="right">7,300</td></tr>
<tr><td>Denmark</td><td align="right">7,250</td></tr>
<tr><td>Bulgaria</td><td align="right">7,000</td></tr>
<tr><td>Turkey</td><td align="right">7,000</td></tr>
<tr><td>Peru</td><td align="right">6,600</td></tr>
<tr><td>Span. Morocco</td><td align="right">5,000</td></tr>
</table>

Total of these 36 countries   17,282,000

In 70 other countries 59,000

Est. World Pop.
of Jews   17,341,000

It is of interest to note that of approximately 17,000,000 Jews, about 80,000 only are resident in Islamic countries; also, that about 3,300,000 are living under Marxist governments; 3,800,000 are in Israel; and finally that about 10,000,000 are resident in countries where Christianity is the dominant religion. These figures could initiate an interesting political-religious discussion in your history classes and current-events clubs.

Chapter VIII

The Dark Continent of Africa

Viewed from an American high school in the waning years of the twentieth century, the vast region that embraces Europe, the Mediterranean Sea, the Near and Middle East, and the continent of Africa is a confusing and mind-baffling challenge. Before we approach consideration of the religions of the Far East, we must update the political and territorial changes that have occurred east of longitudinal meridian zero (Greenwich mean time!).

Already in your minds, I assume, is an outline of the jostling of the Jewish people with the pagans and the Moslems for a national identity and survival. With the entrance of Jesus, the Nazarene, upon the scene as we change B.C. to A.D., the third element of a continuing conflict is recognized.

Within a period of 2500 years, national Judaism had fallen prey to the Persians, the Babylonians, the Greeks, and the Romans. Christianity and Mohammedanism had been contending for the domination of Europe and North Africa. Christianity had won in Europe; Islam had become the prevailing influence in the Near and Middle East and in North Africa. Those ancient tribes, descended in direct line from Abraham, Isaac, Moses, and David, had been scattered over the face of the earth. They had endured the persecutions by both Moslems and Christians. The struggle for Jerusalem had closed after 200 years of bloody crusading.

We have sketched the progress of Europe's conquest of the American continents and we have noted how the Portuguese had examined in a peripheral way the coastline of Africa. Now we return to take a look in some depth at this enormous body of land.

Africa is 11,500,000 square miles—three and one-half times the area of the United States! Its massive body shares the vagaries of global weather from 35° N. Latitude to 35° S. Latitude. From "head to toe" it measures nearly five thousand miles, and between its outstretched "finger tips" lie 4000 more. The world-circling belt of the tropics is wholly contained across its midriff with much to spare above and below. From the glacial heights of Mt. Kilimanjaro to the steamy tropical jungles and sun-scorched deserts, Africa can match the natural wonders to be seen elsewhere in the world.

Return in time to A.D. 1500. Within the perimiters just described were an estimated 130,000,000 men, women, and children. That represented a density of population to the square mile of fourteen. (Compare that with our own 1984 density of sixty-four to the square mile.) The overwhelming majority had no knowledge of that amazing cultural segment in the far northeast corner of the continent that had fully matched the accomplishments of the Greeks and the Romans in the arts, architecture, and science.

Their skin tones ranged from ebony black through shades of brown. Tribally organized, they dwelt in tropical forests or nomadically wandered across the broad savannas and burning sands. Although speaking a hundred different languages, they could neither read nor write. There were no written languages. To survive, they augmented the bounties of nature by spearing or trapping among the world's largest concentration of animal life. Their thatched huts and encircling hedges of thorn bushes provided protection from the elements and minimum security for their domesticated animals. Intertribal warfare and negotiated tribal alliances both destroyed and preserved human life.

They indulged in ceremonial dances, painted and scarified their bodies, and initiated their pubescent youth into the rites of marriage and the lineal succession of family and village authority. It was what one might describe as "slow-motion life," comparable by analogy to time-lapse photography that permits one to watch the emergence of blossom from the planted seed.

Then, quite suddenly, as historical time moves, came a remarkable change. It is time for another intermission. The stage properties must be changed. This is not the same theater in which Moses had made such a name for himself three thousand years earlier. The buzzer sounds, and we enter the auditorium. From our seats in the dress circle, we note that the stage appears newer and less abused than was that older one near Jerusalem. As we turn to scan the reassembling guests, we catch sight of a small cluster of people resuming their balcony seats.

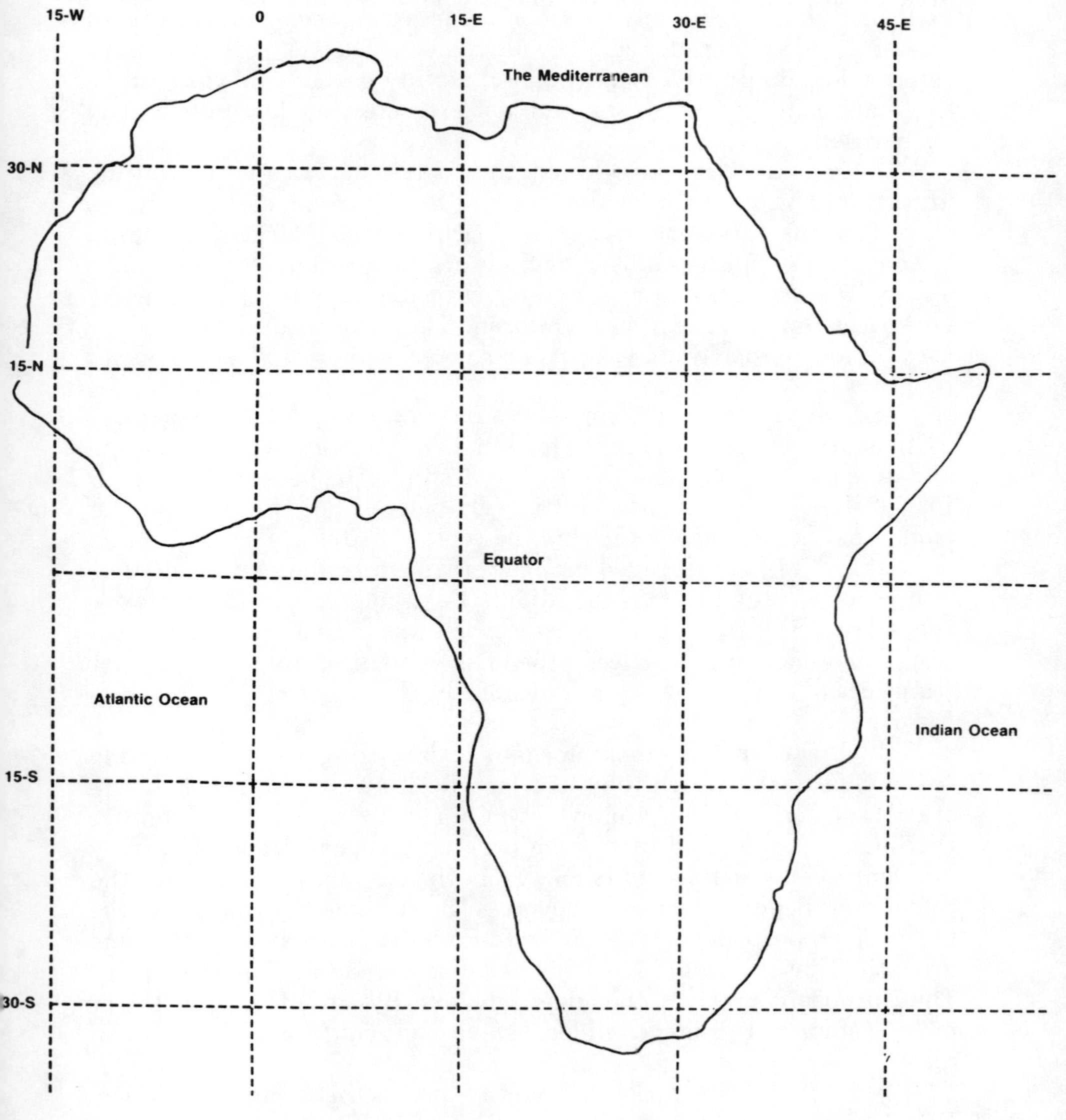

Suggestion: As you read this text, try to locate some of the important points with pencil marks.

No novices are they! They are obviously season ticket-holders. We recognize some of the faces—Isaac and Sarah, Caesar, Barabbas, and Pontius Pilate. Higher up in some of the less expensive seats are Paul, Thomas, Judas Iscariot, and Mary Magdalene. The last person to enter the row is a diminutive little woman, plainly garbed and clutching a tiny handbag from which she had just extracted her last mite to pay for her seat.

The curtain rises. On the apron of the stage is a gesticulating, argumentative group of Portuguese and Moslem traders. Listening to them is a tall, rather handsome, and richly garbed African chieftain. Is he perhaps slightly amused by their argumentation? Behind him is a stack of ivory tusks, and off to the right a dejected, bewildered party of African men, women, and children. They are securely united by cords of agave rope wound about their necks and arms. The story goes like this:

The world time-clock stands at A.D. 1442. King John of Portugal, a Christian nation, has honored his son, Prince Henry, with a dukedom and some authority. The prince loved ships. He became known as Prince Henry the Navigator. Fifty years before Columbus set sails for America, his men were exploring the coasts of Africa. For some years past, they had been engaged in Mediterranean trading with the Moslem peoples, ranging from the Middle East and Egypt all the way to the Atlantic Ocean. Out of this association was to come one of the most tragic and enduring practices—the enslavement of human beings for transport to the developing colonies in the Americas of the Christian European nations.

Much earlier, the Mohammedans, capitalizing upon the existing tribal rivalries of which they had long been aware, gained the cooperation of various chieftains who would set fire to a village, capture the fleeing people, and turn them over to European traders. Slavery had long been practised by Islam. From the east they had invaded the Sudan and begun a lucrative business "back home" by taking blacks to the Arab peoples of the Near and Middle East. In at least this one area, the Christians and Moslems had discovered terms of agreement! The Europeans proved to be adept scholars. By A.D. 1445, some thirty to forty ships were engaged in local slave capturing along the Guinean coast.

By 1502, the navigational "freeway" across the Atlantic was open. You students who have seen the award-winning *Roots* in theater or on television have been introduced to this colossal tragedy not as participants but as serious entertainment.

By 1516, black slaves were being crowded into the holds of ships belonging to the British, the French, the Spanish, and the Dutch. The expanding colonial holdings of the European nations needed low-cost labor to serve the white man's fields, mines, factories, and households. The volume expanded. Between 1680 and 1786, an estimated 2,130,000 slaves had been imported into the American colonies alone. That is an annual average of 20,000. At the time of the American Revolution, more than 200 ships were registered in the slave trade. Along the African coastline were some forty "pick-up stations." Fifteen were Dutch; 14 were British; 4 were Danish; 4 were Portuguese; and 3 were French.

When one learns that almost 50 percent of this human cargo never survived the rigors of capture and transportation, he is stunned by the realization of the destruction of human lives attributable to the followers of the Christian and Islamic faiths. As I sit here at the typewriter, I must pause for a few moments—figuratively, to catch my breath—as I record once again these incredible bits of human history. How could man through stupidity and greed have fallen so far from his declared commitment to a just, compassionate, and merciful God?

Yes, the slave trade was indeed good business! Between 1690 and 1820, more than 800,000 black slaves were sent to Jamaica alone. Between 1680 nd 1700, one licensed company transported 140,000 negroes. Competing, nonauthorized companies carried at least 160,000 more—300,000 in 20 years!

In marching the captives from the hinterlands to the "pick-up" ports, traders needed no guideposts. The trails were strewn with the bones of those who could not endure the stress. It has also been estimated that about 4 percent of all captured blacks died of fright and ill treatment before they could be put aboard ships. More than 12 percent died aboard ship enroute. Thirty percent did not survive the marketing places. Only about half of the captives ever reached their working conditions in the colonies of the western world.

Ahead is a much simplified map of the navigational achievements of the Portuguese. If you have the interest, you can supplement these trade routes of the Portuguese by filling in those of the Dutch, the French, the British, the Spanish, the Germans, and the Danes. This will call for some research in your school library, but you might find this to be challenging.

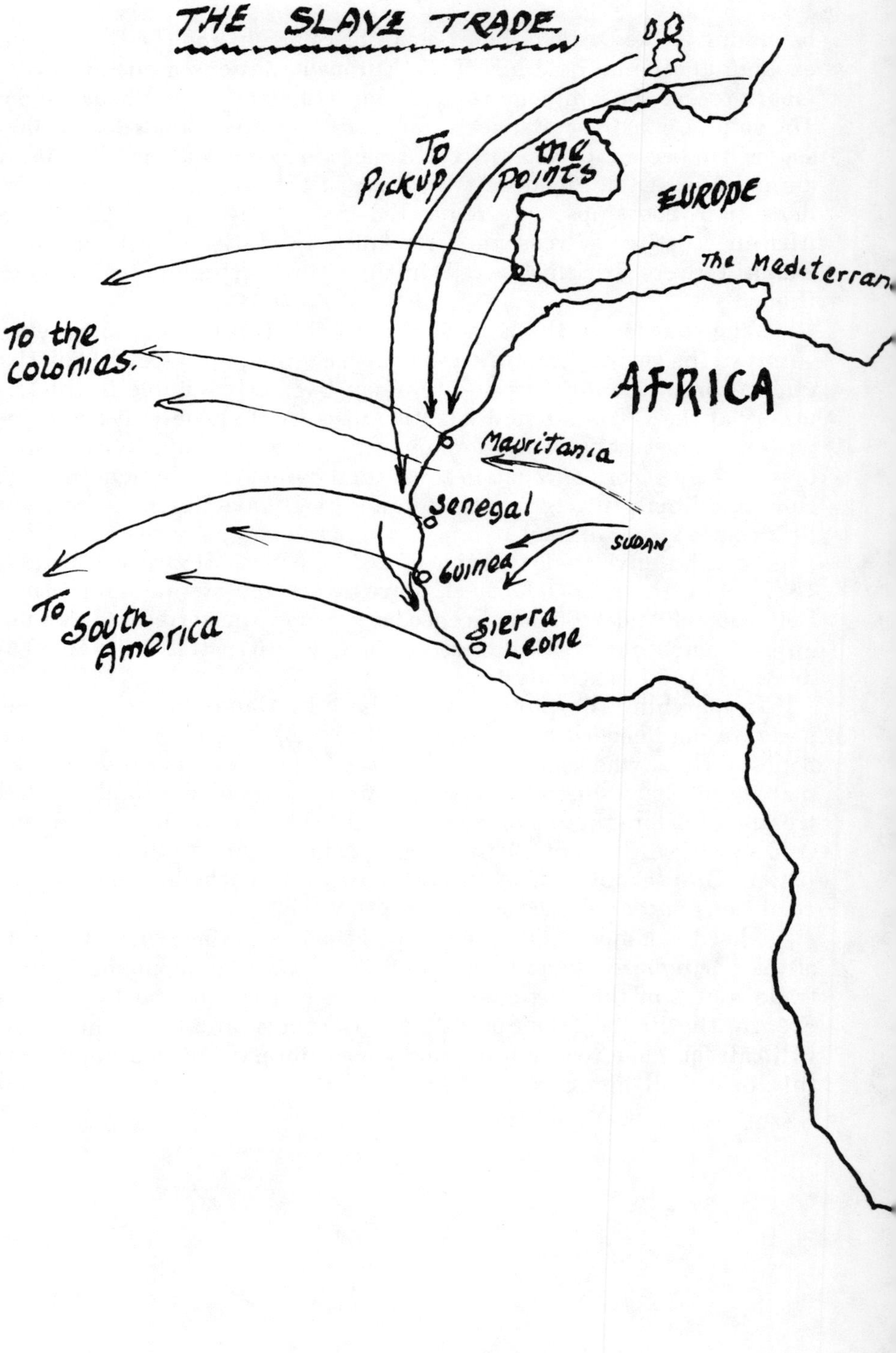

THE SLAVE TRADE
To Pickup the Points
EUROPE
The Mediterranean
To the colonies.
AFRICA
Mauritania
Senegal
SUDAN
Guinea
To South America
Sierra Leone

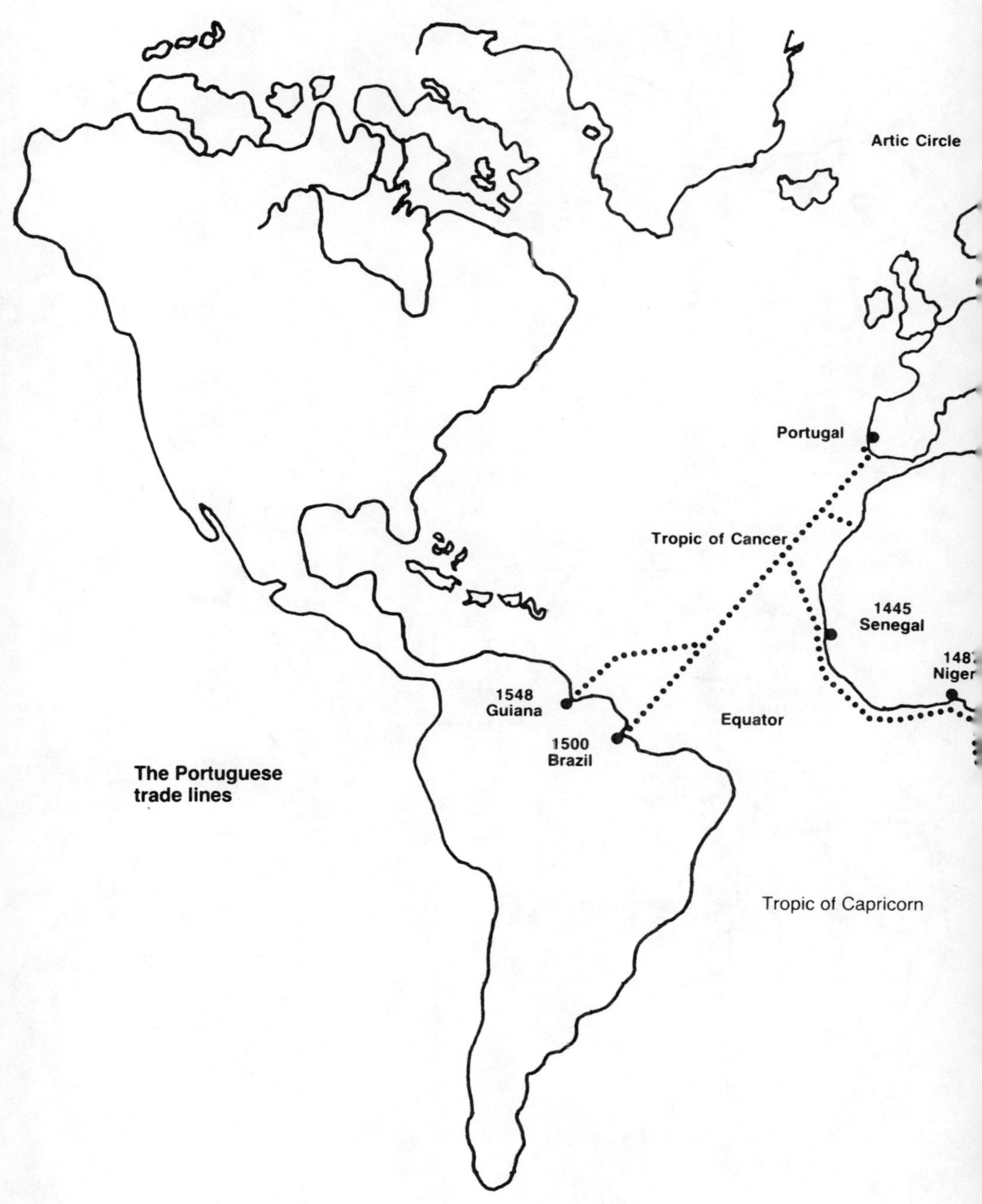

Artic Circle
Portugal
Tropic of Cancer
1445
Senegal
1487
Niger
1548
Guiana
1500
Brazil
Equator
The Portuguese
trade lines
Tropic of Capricorn

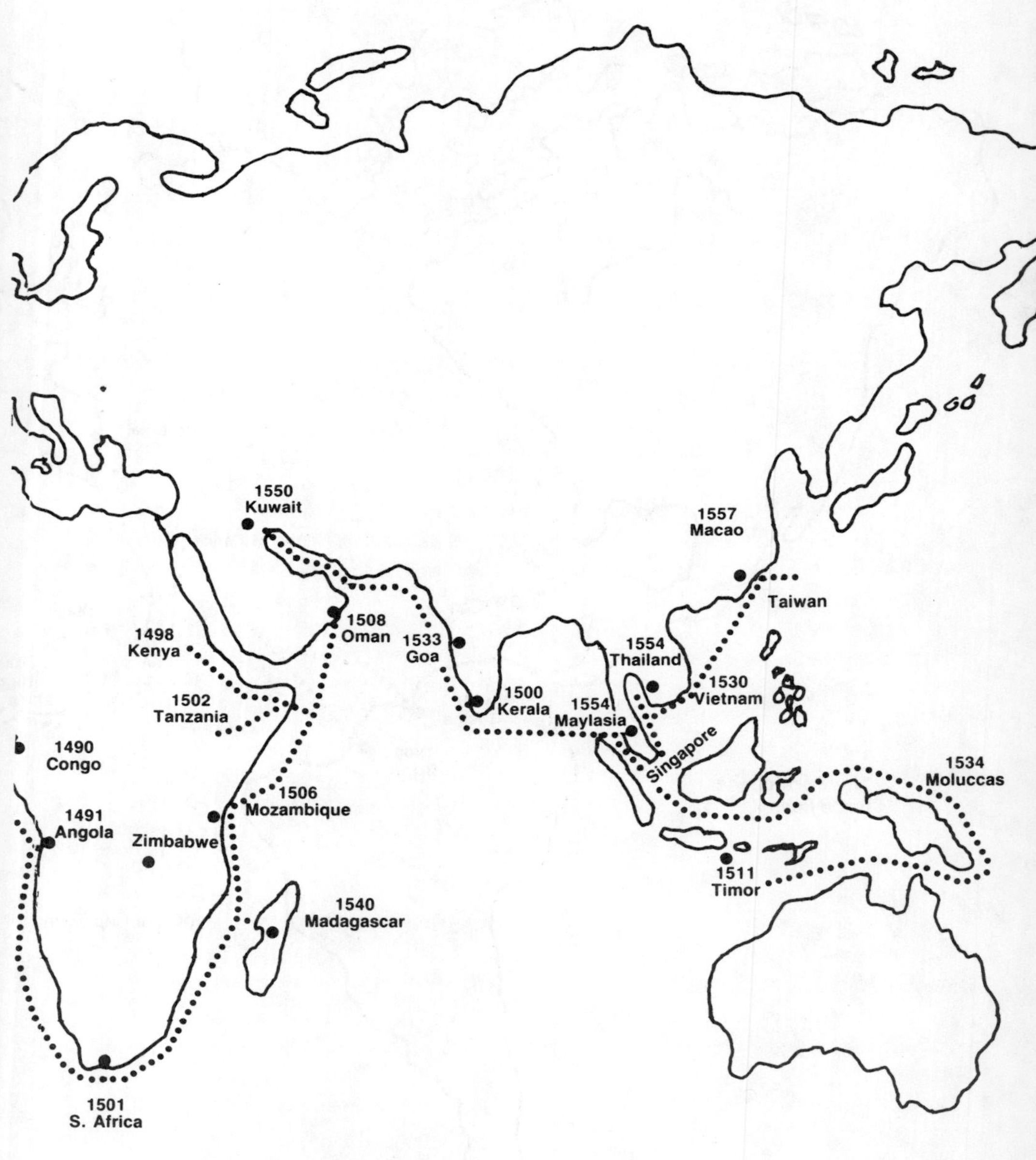

1550
Kuwait
1557
Macao
Taiwan
1498
Kenya
1508
Oman
1533
Goa
1554
Thailand
1530
Vietnam
1502
Tanzania
1500
Kerala
1554
Maylasia
Singapore
1490
Congo
1534
Moluccas
1491
Angola
Zimbabwe
1506
Mozambique
1511
Timor
1540
Madagascar
1501
S. Africa

Chapter IX

The Brighter Side

My maternal grandfather, a twenty-three–year–old Swiss immigrant, worked as a blacksmith and carriage builder in Louisville, Kentucky. The year was 1861. On business he had gone to New Orleans. While standing in a public market square, he witnessed what, to him, was unbelievable: an auctioneer offering to the highest bidders the black slaves of the white man—men, women, and children. His techniques of persuasion were identical with other auctioneers selling cattle, horses, and pigs in the same marketplace.

So shocked was he by this inhuman activity that he resolved to do what he could to fight the practice upon his return home to that border state. Unfortunately, his plan was temporarily postponed when he was impressed into service by the army of the seceding Confederate States.

With a companion, he escaped the pursuing posse several weeks later, joined the Union army, and served until the war's conclusion. Clearly do I remember how, as a boy of nine, I sat spellbound by his description of man's inhumanity to man. The Civil War, he said, and its resultant bloodshed, was God's punishment for the enslavement of His black children. All were guilty, both North and South, and the "sins of the father were being visited upon the children" of the next generations.

My grandfather's protest, long after the freeing of the slaves, was but an echo of the widespread Christian revulsion against the slave trade that marked 200 years of our history. This is "the brigher side." From the vantage point of 1986, the confrontations of the slave-trading years seem endless. Concerned Christians, both in government and without, knew that the barbaric practice must go. The problem would have to be resolved in two stages: 1. stopping the traffic, and 2. granting emancipation from slavery to political freedom.

How slowly the international wheels of justice turn is reflected in the 200 years required to remove, by official acts of government, the scourge of trading in human beings. Denmark took the first action by a royal decree of May 16, 1792, that all such traffic must cease by the year 1802. Our young United States forbade our ships to engage in the slave trade in 1794, but not until 1807 did we stop their importation. As you students are aware, our slave population was given freedom status on February 1, 1865. It required the passage of the Thirteenth and Fifteenth Amendments to the Constitution (1865 and 1870) to define sharply our obligation to the black people. By that time, we were setting free the children and grandchildren of those who had originally arrived as captive beings.

Although such terms as *slave*, *slavery*, and *slave traffic* appear at no point in our Constitution, our Founding Fathers made certain that the evil was doomed by the insertion of the First Amendment and the Bill of Rights. Despite the progress of the western world in checking this heinous business, the trade was carried on for years by smugglers who were not the least interested in having their profitable venture terminated. Any hope that the European nations held that the task was finished was banished by another extension of slavery.

Unlike the Christian tradition of extending Love to all fellow human beings, the *Koran* of Mohammedanism recognized slavery as a legitimate segment of the organized society. The old Judaic code was also tolerant. In neither society was there an ethical code that was opposed to slavery and the slave trade. If you will turn to the detailed treatment of slavery to be found in the *Encyclopaedia Britannica*, this is what you will read:

After the trade in slaves to America and the West Indies from West Africa had been declared illegal in the early part of the nineteenth century, a very considerable amount of smuggling traffic was carried on until slavery was abolished in America. . . . The term "slave trade" now bore a new meaning as referring either to the surreptitious export of slaves to Persia, Arabia, and the Red Sea littoral from the northeast and eastern coasts of the continent, or from the internal slave trade to satisfy the demands of the Mohammedan states in the north and west of Zanzibar, as well as the Negro kingdoms of Uganda, Benin, and Dahomey. Of the slaves required by the latter, large numbers were sacrificed in Pagan ceremonies or upon the death of the King or their owners.

The central Sudan appeared to be one vast hunting ground. Captives were brought thence to the slave market of Kuka in Bornu, where, after being bought by dealers, they were to the number of about 10,000 annually marched across the Sahara to Murzuk in Fezzan, from which place they were distributed to the northern and eastern Mediterranean coasts. Their sufferings were dreadful; many succumbed and were abandoned.

Negroes were also brought to Morocco from the western Sudan and forwarded to a great yearly fair. [From there] the slaves were forwarded in gangs to Marrakesh, Fez, and Maquinez. About 4,000 were annually thus imported, and an "ad valorem" duty was levied by the Sultan. . . .

The basin of the Upper Nile . . . was another region infested by the slave trade; the slaves were either smuggled into Egypt or sent by the Red Sea to Turkey. The eventual control of the African slave trade was brought about in the nineteenth century by the takeover by European Christians of most of the continent of Africa.

Consider another quotation from the same source:

The second phase of the slave trade, viz . . . the raids for slaves to supply internal demands from Mohammedan states, was, of course, doomed to extinction. . . . The consolidation of French rule in the north . . . and the final defeat of powerful potentates in the west put an end to the organized traffic, although as late as 1926 parties of tribesmen in the deserts still defied authority.

In Nigeria, the power of the Mohammedan rulers who annually employed large armies in raiding for slaves had depopulated great regions. [This was] broken in 1902–1903.

In the Congo region, King Leopold (Belgium) declared war . . . on the east-coast Arabs who had settled there and become powerful despots—independent of Zanzibar. In Nyasaland, a favorite hunting ground of Zanzibar slavers . . . the control was assumed by Great Britain. Before the close of the first decade of the twentieth century, a more or less effective administration had been established throughout Africa under European control.

As late as 1926, the newly formed League of Nations, following the Treaty of Versailles after World War I, in convention assembled, submitted a proposal to bring about "progressively as soon as possible the complete abolition of slavery in all its forms." At the 1927 convention of the assembly, every colonial power agreed to ratify the proposal "at an early date." The United States was not signatory to the League of Nations, which was superseded in 1945 by the United Nations Organization in San Francisco, California.

***

What you have just been reading about slavery represents no original research on my part. The purpose in assembling these facts from the vast sources available is to bring into focus the inescapable relationship between man's religions and his secular history. In the earlier pages you noted the Founding Fathers' testimony to dependence upon God. As we continue our study, embracing the colonization of Africa during the nineteenth century, *we should keep in mind that the abolition of slavery came from the recognition by Christian people that what they had been doing was intolerable among those who were committed to a moral code and a Supreme Being.* Out of the anguish of restitution came an example for the oppressed people of the world of a nation committed to freedom. The United States was a Christian nation. Without the presence of a state church, its people had risen to the spiritual motivation of an accepted moral code.

Immediately following are three additional maps. Please do not turn quickly through them. They are extremely important if you are to grasp the full significance of the century of your grandparents. Something very dramatic was happening on a scale not heretofore seen in world history. And keep in mind also that while the colonization of Africa was being accomplished, the same urge to expand trade to the Far East had gone on almost simultaneously. We shall be coming to that when we take up the religions of the Far East. What you may have sensed so far of the interlocking of religions and political history is but a small portion of what we still are to encounter.

Suggested Research Topics

1. World Trade in the Seventeenth and Eighteenth Centuries
2. Public Statements by Government Officials with Regard to the Slave Trade
3. The Varieties of Tribal Organization in Africa
4. How Trading Companies Handled Their Products
5. Labor Conditions of Slaves in the Americas

90

6. Leaders of the Abolition Movement
7. Revolts among the Enslaved Population
8. The Aftereffects of World Slavery
9. International Competition in the Slave Trade
10. The Fusion of Indian-Black Cultures

Now that we have summarized the involvement of the predominantly Christian nations of Europe in the slave traffic, it is time for another intermission. Those ancient guests who have been watching the production from the balcony seats and from the less expensive ones in the "peanut gallery" have become restless. Moses seems to be walking with a limp, burdened as he is by that clay notebook under one arm—inscribed "The Ten Commandments." Pontius Pilate has slipped into the washroom to rinse his hands in the manner of Lady Macbeth. King David, having caught sight of Uriah the Hittite, purposely avoided an encounter lest Uriah inquire after the health of Bathsheba.

Outside the theater entrance, they mount their assorted camels, donkeys, and chariots. They are obviously upset. They are leaving the historical play. The three disciples are accosted by the doorman.

"You're not leaving, are you? This is only an intermission. The next act is one of the most dramatic!"

"Well, you see," responded Paul, stamping the dust of the street from his sandals, "We're disappointed. All our preaching to the Gentiles some 1500 years ago doesn't seem to have done much good. Furthermore, we like the old theater in Jerusalem much more than this one. That's where we had some pretty fine contacts with the churches of Corinth. We're all going home."

It was at that precise moment that Pontius Pilate, wrapping his toga about him and about to set foot in his chariot, caught the drift of Paul's remarks. "Oh, I say, young men—I'm Pontius Pilate. I hope you chaps do not still carry a grudge against me for what happened that day on Golgotha. I did my best to save your leader and to quiet the crowd, but they insisted on my releasing Barabbas. I lost all track of him after that."

Peter cut in at that point. "Listen, Pontius, that's your problem. You're going to have to live with it. In a way, I sympathize with you. I made a couple—or was it three?—bad mistakes in my time. I know what you're going through."

"Thanks. I just wanted to know how you felt. I've got to be going myself. Sorry there's no room for you fellows in my chariot. Just me and my driver."

The camel-donkey caravan was already far down the road. The buzzer sounded for the continuation of the play. As the remaining guests sought their seats, one was heard to remark: "I wonder if we'll ever get to the final act. I have the feeling that this play is going to go on forever!"

***

With that little interlude, we consider the African continent from another angle. What had been going on there for several centuries under the operational tactics of the European Christian nations came suddenly to an end, as historical times goes. The three maps which follow show the drastic changes following World War I and World War II. Read very carefully the textual material accompanying the three maps. The class will also do well to study in detail the original charter proclamation of the United Nations Organization as set forth in 1945.

Africa in 1914

Here is the evidence that, at the beginning of World War I, the "Christian" nations of Europe had been extraordinarily successful in taking control, either through colonization or "protectorate status" of the entire continent of Africa *with the exception of Liberia and Abyssinia.*

Within a period of 400 years, (1500–1900), Great Britain, France, Germany, Italy, Belgium, Spain, and Portugal moved in on 11,000,000 square miles of country loosely belonging to about 130,000,000 tribal peoples, largely negroid, and began exploiting the natural resources of the lands they had stolen.

Among these seven nations, there were many conflicts, many hastily constructed treaties, many adjustments in boundary lines.

Although Islam had earlier taken over most of North Africa and thus introduced the Mohammedan faith, the many religious Moslems were under the political control of France, Italy, and Great Britain.

It was out of this setting that the above Christian countries became involved in the slave trade when the Mohammedan traders, working with tribal chieftains, acquainted the Portuguese with the profits to be made by selling black human beings to the new colonies in the Americas.

92

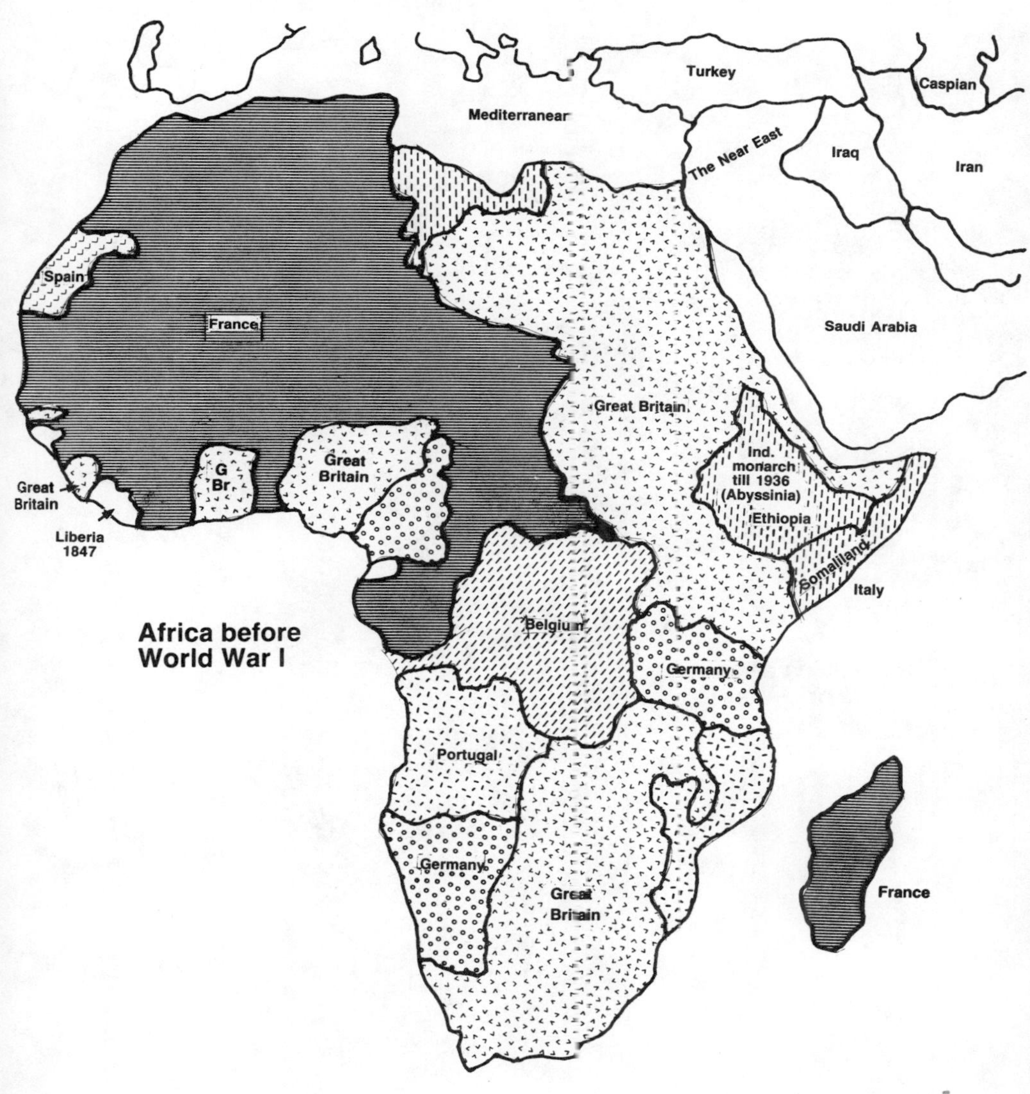

Africa before World War I

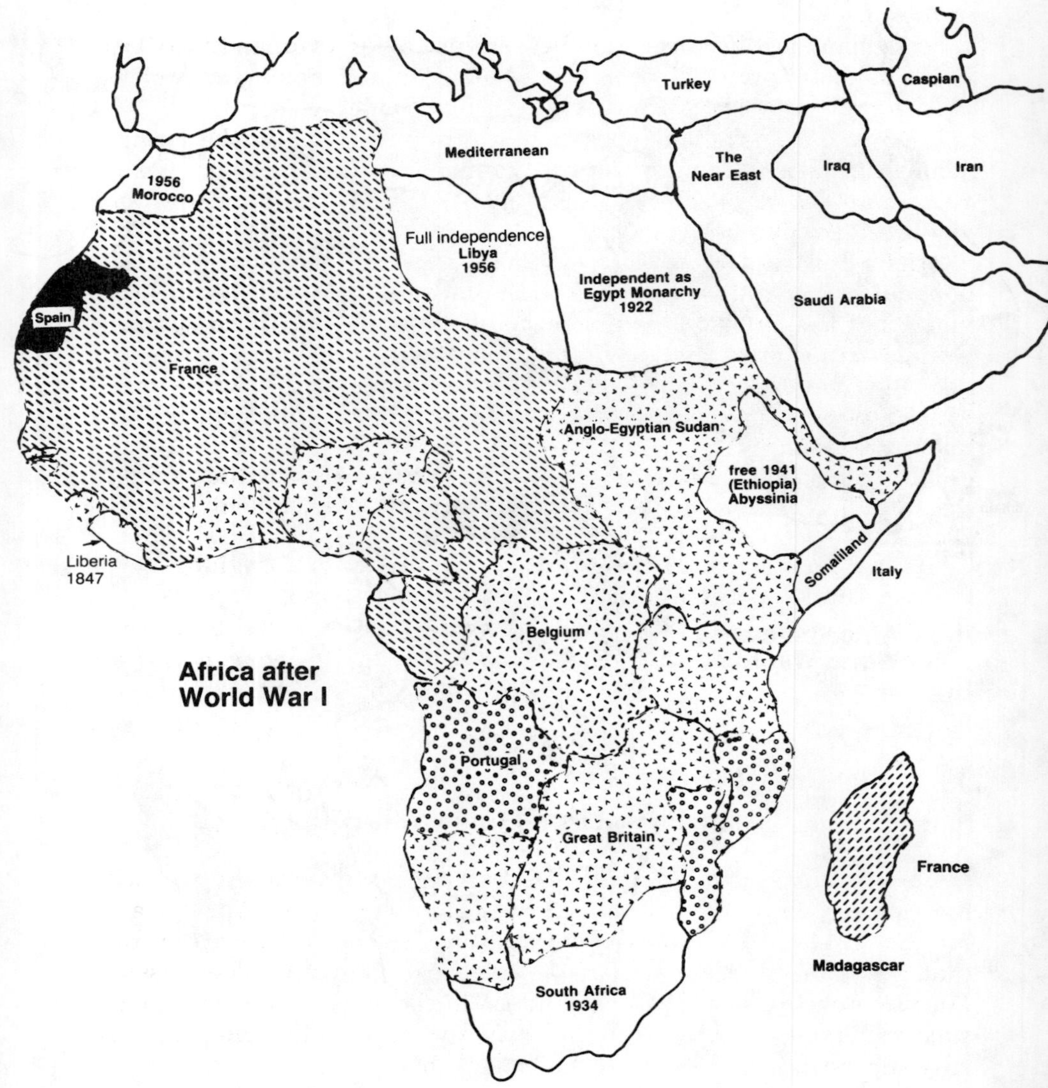

Turkey
Caspian
Mediterranean
The Near East
Iraq
Iran
1956 Morocco
Full independence Libya 1956
Independent as Egypt Monarchy 1922
Saudi Arabia
Spain
France
Anglo-Egyptian Sudan
free 1941 (Ethiopia) Abyssinia
Liberia 1847
Belgium
Somaliland
Italy
Africa after World War I
Portugal
Great Britain
France
Madagascar
South Africa 1934

Africa After World War I

The defeat of Germany and the ambivalence of Italy in the "War to preserve civilization" brought significant changes in political controls in Africa.

Germany lost her three colonies (see preceding map) and Italy lost Libya to a joint protectorate of France and England. Somaliland fell to British protection in 1927 until its later independence.

Egypt and Libya had new boundary lines established; the former achieving national status from its protectorate status under Great Britain. It also moved into joint-administratioin with England over the whole Sudan area below Libya.

As a result of World I, great changes were also effected in the boundaries and controls among the European countries. It became obvious that the long domination of the black peoples of Africa by their European masters would inevitably change as the colonized peoples of ancient tribal background learned of the techniques of the "white" man which could be applied toward their release from the "imperialism" of several centuries.

Italy turned over to England the Trusteeship of Somaliland after the war. U.N. action in 1949 would make it an independent state in 1950. Italy was reassigned the trusteeship.

It is clear from the typed-in areas, that France and England were the "large landholders" in Africa at that moment.

The next map will bring you to a realization of how the alignment of the nations of the world has changed in a relatively short period of time.

Now, Please Don't Be in a Hurry!

If you have carefully examined the two preceding maps, you will have picked up much to stimulate your thinking. When World War I broke out in 1914, the countries of Europe had something to worry about that was more important than their colonies in Africa. The Russian Marxist Revolution of 1917 gave notice to the world that communism was laying its future plans to take over the world and to rid it of that silly superstition that religion was important.

While the free world was pondering how to handle that threat, Adolf Hitler was designing a new future for the German people, the horror of which the world could not even anticipate. In that relatively

short time-span of twenty-five years, even the colonies became concerned lest their fairly orderly lives be interrupted by a political upheaval that was incomprehensible to them. Maybe the life in the
colonies was no so bad after all.

Then the feared war came! In fact, much use was made of colonial
resources, including military personnel. What was happening in Europe was also threatening to occur in the Far Eastern colonies of the
French and the Dutch. What would happen if the European guardians
were defeated?

As the war broadened to involve the United States and Japan, the
latent threats of revolution against the colonial masters were put on
the shelf for the time being. With World War II's successful conclusion,
however, thoughts of eventual release from colonial status to one of
self-determination grew into a chorus of protests. The colonials wanted
freedom from being "owned by someone else."

In a very general way, you have studied this in your classes in
American and European history. You may recall the colorful person,
Mahatma Gandhi, who moved about in Africa before World War II,
stirring up the patriotic senses of the many Hindus who were living
there; you learned of his imprisonment, subsequent release, and the
honors that came to him when India received its freedom from British
rule at the war's close (1947).

The colonial governments of Europe were faced with the rebuilding
of their economies; in many ways, colonial ownership prevented a quick
recovery. Furthermore, the tide of unrest now had opportunity to express openly the determination to be free. Suddenly the colonial system
came to an end. No one of the five remaining European countries that
held colonies was granted any delaying action of significance. This you
will fix in mind when you analyse the otherwise confusing third map.

A further word about the last map: On it are listed forty-five countries within the actual coastline of the continent of Africa. Added to
those are countries of the Near and Middle East that are so intimately
related to what is going on in that area today. Seventy-four of the
region's countries with membership in the United Nations are thus
listed, including the forty-five that are exclusively African.

With the granting of freedom, the main objective of the newly
independent peoples was to establish a working government and to
apply for membership in the United Nations. The charts that immediately follow will show how incredibly fast those objectives were accomplished.

The several statistical charts that follow are related exclusively
to the forty-five countries that lie within the coastline of the continent

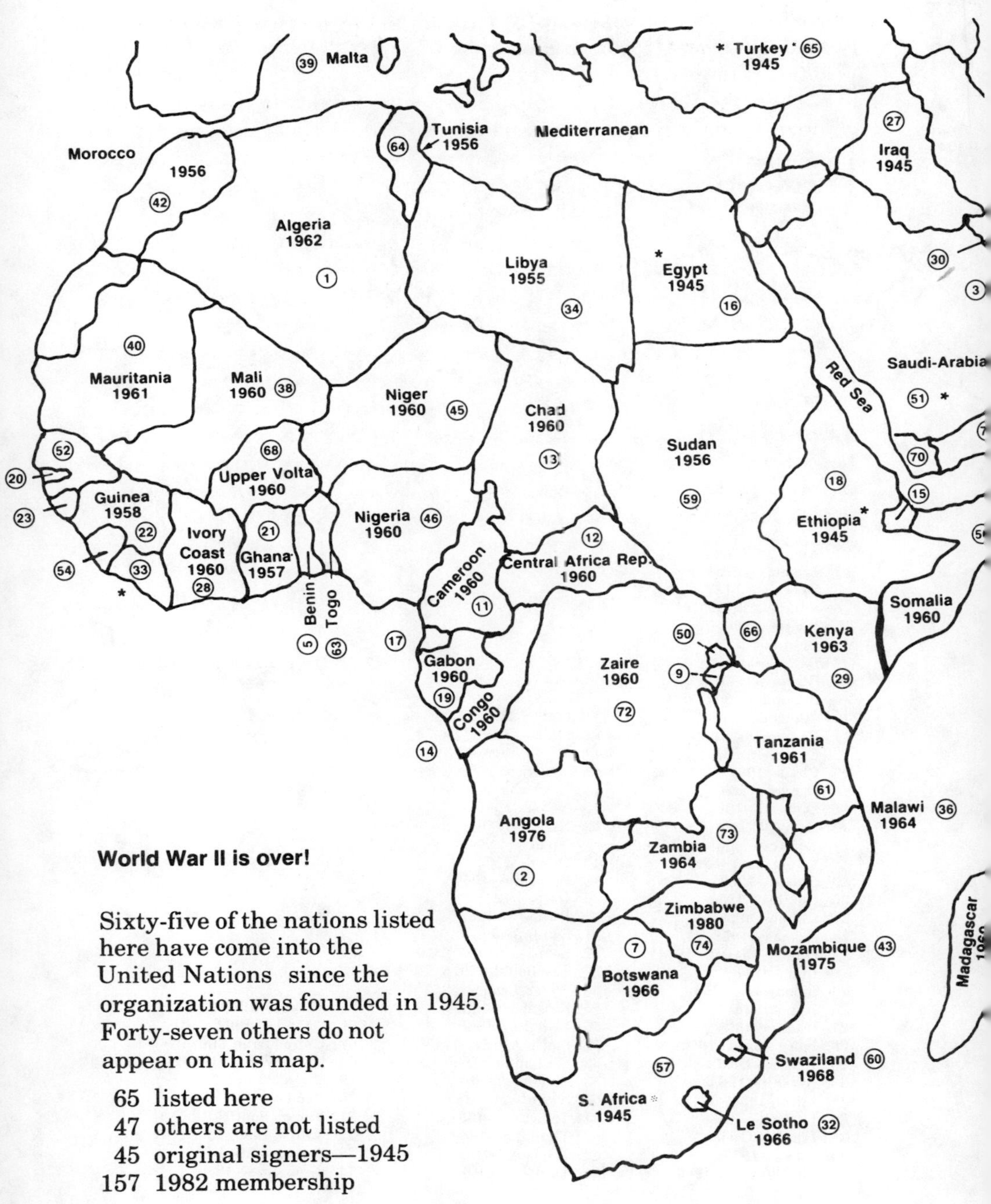

World War II is over!

Sixty-five of the nations listed here have come into the United Nations since the organization was founded in 1945. Forty-seven others do not appear on this map.

65 listed here
47 others are not listed
45 original signers—1945
157 1982 membership

*Members of the United Nations Organization of 1945

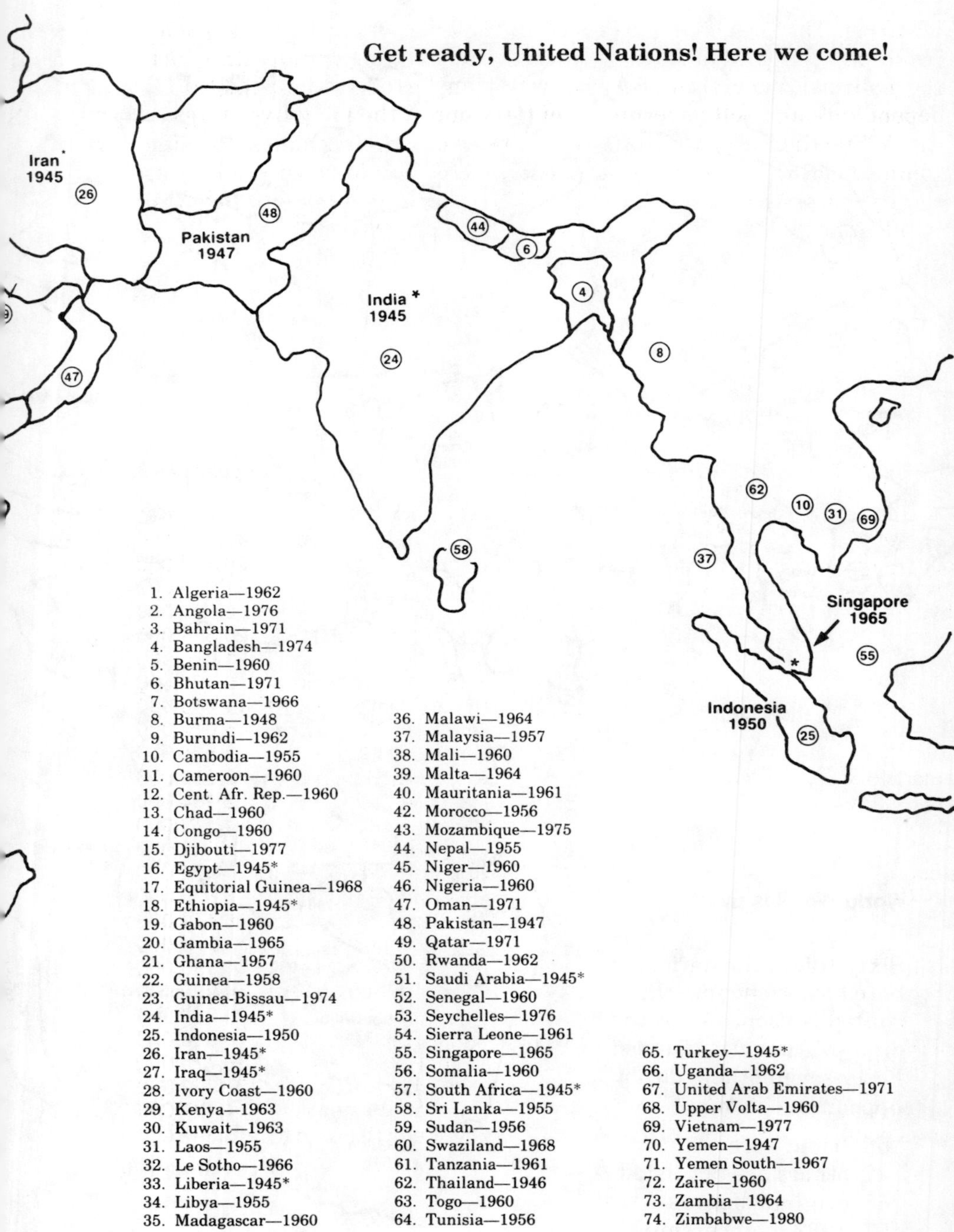

Get ready, United Nations! Here we come!

1. Algeria—1962
2. Angola—1976
3. Bahrain—1971
4. Bangladesh—1974
5. Benin—1960
6. Bhutan—1971
7. Botswana—1966
8. Burma—1948
9. Burundi—1962
10. Cambodia—1955
11. Cameroon—1960
12. Cent. Afr. Rep.—1960
13. Chad—1960
14. Congo—1960
15. Djibouti—1977
16. Egypt—1945*
17. Equitorial Guinea—1968
18. Ethiopia—1945*
19. Gabon—1960
20. Gambia—1965
21. Ghana—1957
22. Guinea—1958
23. Guinea-Bissau—1974
24. India—1945*
25. Indonesia—1950
26. Iran—1945*
27. Iraq—1945*
28. Ivory Coast—1960
29. Kenya—1963
30. Kuwait—1963
31. Laos—1955
32. Le Sotho—1966
33. Liberia—1945*
34. Libya—1955
35. Madagascar—1960

36. Malawi—1964
37. Malaysia—1957
38. Mali—1960
39. Malta—1964
40. Mauritania—1961
42. Morocco—1956
43. Mozambique—1975
44. Nepal—1955
45. Niger—1960
46. Nigeria—1960
47. Oman—1971
48. Pakistan—1947
49. Qatar—1971
50. Rwanda—1962
51. Saudi Arabia—1945*
52. Senegal—1960
53. Seychelles—1976
54. Sierra Leone—1961
55. Singapore—1965
56. Somalia—1960
57. South Africa—1945*
58. Sri Lanka—1955
59. Sudan—1956
60. Swaziland—1968
61. Tanzania—1961
62. Thailand—1946
63. Togo—1960
64. Tunisia—1956

65. Turkey—1945*
66. Uganda—1962
67. United Arab Emirates—1971
68. Upper Volta—1960
69. Vietnam—1977
70. Yemen—1947
71. Yemen South—1967
72. Zaire—1960
73. Zambia—1964
74. Zimbabwe—1980

of Africa. The first chart, arranged in the order of admission to membership in the United Nations, reveals the startling speed with which the political ownership of Africa was transferred to the political independence and self government of forty-one of the forty-five states.

While the European nations were releasing their colonies, Russian communism was reversing the trend by creating Marxist colonies as rapidly as possible. Note carefully the types of governmental control in effect as of 1984.

Chart I

Country	Independence	United Nations	Gov't 1984	Population
Liberia	1847	1945	Rep. Mil. Junta	1,937,000
Egypt	1922	1945	One Party Soc. St.	42,144,000
South AFrica	1934	1945	Republic	28,533,000
Ethiopia	1941	1945	Soc. Mil. Junta	31,522,000
Libya	1955	1955	Soc. Mil. Junta	2,638,000
Morocco	1956	1956	Const. Monarchy	20,384,000
Sudan	1956	1956	One Party Republic	21,420,000
Tunisia	1956	1956	One Party Republic	6,561,000
Ghana	1957	1957	Military Junta	11,446,000
Guinea	1958	1958	One Party Soc. St.	5,014,000
Benin	1960	1960	Communist	3,534,000
Cameroon	1960	1960	One Party Republic	7,088,000
Cent. Af. Rep.	1960	1960	Republic	2,004,000
Chad	1960	1960	Military Junta	4,473,000
Congo	1960	1960	Communist	1,532,000
Gabon	1960	1960	One Party Republic	546,000
Ivory Coast	1960	1960	One Party Republic	5,579,000
Mali	1960	1960	Mil. Dictatorship	6,470,000
Niger	1960	1960	Military Junta	5,272,000
Nigeria	1960	1960	Federal Republic	72,956,000
Senegal	1960	1960	One Party Republic	4,989,000
Somalia	1960	1960	One Party Soc. St.	3,652,000
Togo	1960	1960	Military Dictator.	2,596,000
Upper Volta	1960	1960	Military Rule	6,774,000
Zaire	1960	1960	One Party Republic	27,952,000
Mauritania	1960	1961	One Party Republic	1,427,000
Sierre Leone	1961	1961	One Party Republic	3,392,000

Tanzania	1961	1961	One Party Soc. Rep.	18,052,000
Algeria	1962	1962	Soc. Mil. Junta	19,828,000
Burundi	1962	1962	Military Junta	4,288,000
Rwanda	1961	1962	Military Rep.	4,865,000
Uganda	1962	1962	MilitaryRep.	13,222,000
Kenya	1963	1963	One Party Republic	15,688,000
Malawi	1963	1964	One party Republic	5,577,000
Zambia	1964	1964	One Party Republic	5,875,000
Gambia	1965	1965	Parlia. Republic	563,000
Botswana	1966	1966	Republic	795,000
Lesotho	1966	1966	Parl. Const. Monarch	1,284,000
Equ. Guinea	1966	1968	Dictatorship	339,000
Swaziland	1968	1968	Absolute Monarchy	543,000
Guinea-Bisseau	1973	1974	Mil. Soc. State	573,000
Mozambique	1975	1975	Communist	10,375,000
Angola	1975	1976	Communist	7,181,000
Djibouti	1977	1977	Republic	119,000
Zimbabwe	1965	1980	Parlia. Republic	7,495,000

1980 Population = 448,497,000
Estimated 1500 Population = 138,000,000

Population Growth = 318,497,000

SUMMARIZING STATEMENT

The three charts which follow may prove to be the most interesting and the most informative among the many to which you are being subjected. Most of the countries listed above experienced steadily increasing pressures and then final takeover by the "Christian" nations of Europe. The movement began slowly with the "Age of Exploration" about A.D. 1500 and expired following World War II about A.D. 1950 —roughly a period of four hundred fifty years.

Prior to the "Age of Exploration," only vestiges of the earlier Christian implantation survived the onrush of armed Mohammedanism across the whole of North Africa. All would change with the entry of Christian Europe into political control of most of the African continent.

Below you will find a regrouping of the forty-five nations above with reference to the population dominance of Christians, Moslems, or Tribalists.

Chart II Christian Population Largest

COUNTRY	CHRISTIANS	MOSLEMS	TRIBALISTS	GOV'T.
Angola	6,453,000	00,000,000	684,000	Communist
Botswana	399,000	260	391,000	Republic
Burundi	3,666,000	39,000	580,000	Military
Cameroon	3,936,000	1,559,000	1,531,000	Republic
Cen. Af. Rep.	1,693,000	64,000	240,000	Republic
Congo	1,425,000	6,500	73,000	Communist
Eq. Guinea	301,000	1,550	15,600	Dictatorship
Ethiopia	17,967,000	9,898,000	3,605,000	Soc. Military
Gabon	525,000	4,400	15,800	Republic
Ghana	7,165,000	1,797,000	2,451,000	Military
Kenya	11,452,000	941,300	2,972,000	Republic
Lesotho	1,192,000	640	80,200	Monarchy
Malawi	3,597,000	903,500	1,057,400	Republic
Nigeria	35,572,000	32,668,000	4,100,000	Republic
Rwandi	3,551,000	420,000	885,200	Military
S. Africa	22,598,000	362,000	4,534,000	Republic
Swaziland	418,000	400	113,490	Monarchy
Tanzania	7,943,000	5,867,000	4,155,000	Socialist
Uganda	10,353,000	872,000	1,661,000	Republic
Zaire	26,414,000	390,000	955,420	Republic
Zimbabwe	4,347,000	70,000	3,034,000	Republic
	170,977,000	55,865,000	33,134,000	

Chart III Moslem Population Largest

COUNTRY	CHRISTIANS	MOSLEMS	TRIBALISTS	GOV'T
Algeria	152,000	19,640,000	000000000	Military
Chad	1,476,000	1,968,000	1,020,000	Military
Djibouti	10,400	108,000	000000000	Republic
Egypt	7,514,000	34,468,000	000000000	Socialist
Gambia	18,700	477,200	61,900	Republic
Guinea	65,000	3,460,000	1,481,260	Socialist
Libya	45,200	2,589,000	000000000	Military
Mali	120,000	5,179,170	1,170,000	Military
Mauritania	16,000	1,419,200	800	Republic
Morocco	102,300	20,256,700	000000000	Monarchy
Niger	14,120	4,635,900	615,880	Military
Senegal	285,000	4,540,370	159,600	Republic
Somalia	2,270	3,643,180	000000000	Socialist
Sudan	1,939,300	15,637,000	3,579,000	Republic
Tunisia	120,000	6,523,120	000000000	Republic
	11,885,000	124,553,000	12,598,000	

COUNTRY	CHRISTIANS	MOSLEMS	TRIBALISTS	GOV'T.
Benin	816,000	357,000	2,170,000	Communist
Guin-Bisseau	58,360	219,000	293,850	Socialist
Ivory Coast	1,785,300	1,339,000	2,442,600	Republic
Liberia	678,000	410,000	843,400	Military
Mozambique	4,035,900	1,349,000	4,963,700	Communist
Sierre Leone	305,300	1,336,400	1,747,150	Republic
Togo	960,500	441,300	1,188,200	Military
Upper Volta	826,400	2,913,000	3,032,900	Military
	9,466,000	8,366,000	16,682,000	

TOTALS	CHRISTIANS	MOSLEMS	TRIBALISTS
	192,328,000	188,784,000	62,414,000

Total Est. African Population =	448,000,000
Total in Three Religious Groups =	443,526,000
The Estimated Remainder =	4,474,000

This latter figure would cover all other persons:
Buddhists, Sikhs, Hindus, Jains, Parsis, Confucianists, Taoists, and Jews.

It seems reasonable to conclude from these African charts that:

1. Christians have overtaken Moslems in population count.
2. Missionary efforts by the Christians of the European nations that colonized Africa were highly successful.
3. Growth of the Christian population was accelerated by missionary efforts from the Americas, especially the United States and Canada during the past one hundred years.
4. Missionaries of Christianity have no shortage of material for their evangelical motivation among the more than 62,000,000 African tribes people!
5. If Christian missionary efforts continue to succeed as in the past, dominant membership volume will soon shift from the white race to the blacks, browns, yellows, and other descriptive groupings.

Well, What Does All This Mean to Us?

This is a more profound question than you may suspect. For some of the younger generation it may be boring. They would prefer a class in modern dance or in the stage acrobatics of guitar playing. History, especially that which involves religion, is for the "old folks" whose days are in need of quiet activity.

There are other young people, however, who look ahead as well as about them. Without discarding the excitement of being young and physically active, they have a curiosity to find answers to the deluge of problems that bother their parents, grandparents, and even some members of the Congress and the President of the United States! This can become an engrossing hobby.

For instance, look again at the listing of seventy-four nations on that last map. Forty-five of them are located within the limits of the African continent. Twenty-nine others are from the Near and Middle East—countries with which we shall soon be concerned again as we move to the religions of the Far East. Who could possibly have predicted the following outcome of the releasing of the African colonies?

Only nineteen of the forty-five African states have adopted governments that can be loosely defined as democracies. They are mostly "One-Party Republics" that tend to stifle the urge to be critical of the acts of government.

Twelve of the forty-five are now under some type of military control, frequently resulting from the seizure of power by force from some initial experiment with democratic methods.

Five announce themselves as socialist states, with plans to improve upon the failures of the free enterprise system.

Three retain old monarchies with modern adjustments.

Four of them have become Communist countries, followers of the Marxist line out of the Russian revolution.

One is an acknowledged Dictator.

One remains an "absolute monarchy."

So, repeating the questions, what does all this mean?

What are the elements behind this diversification of governmental structures?

What will be the influence still to be exerted by the former "owners?"

How will more than 62,000,000 members of Africa's tribal religions be brought into a working relationship with modern education, medicine, and the technologic "fireworks" of the current world?

What pressures will be put upon them in their political innocence by the aggressive moves of communism?

How will they adjust to the new experience of earning a living in an industrial society?

Can they be brought to accept courts of law as replacement for ancient family systems of justice?

Without the use of much imagination, we can see that questions like those above will appear endlessly as man struggles to meet the challenges arising from this one small segment of international upheaval. How many changes will precede your reading this page?

And don't neglect to keep in mind that *Communism is just as much a religion as Mohammedanism and Christianity.* It seeks to destroy the latter; that the *Moslem world is opposed to Communism, but also discourages the presence of other religions when it holds governmental authority. Christianity offers freedom to worship* and to propagate one's religion without interference from governmental authority. It is the dominance of the Christian faith among the citizens of our country that conditions the life and conduct of our officials. No organized religious group tells us how to run our country. We, the franchised voters, still retain that authority. As a nation of Christians we've done fairly well so far. Make a list of the characteristics of our nation of which you approve. Weigh them against what you find elsewhere in the world. Then invite your Moslem, Jewish, and other friends to tell your class in Religions and History about their own religious beliefs and practices. They have the same assured freedom as you. What have we to fear?

Chapter X

A Different Theater with Changes
in the Cast

At this point in your reading, aside from cursory mention of the religions of the Far East, you have been introduced to two of the largest and most active of the living religions of the world—Christianity and Mohammedanism. It is necessary to remind ourselves, however, that *Secular Humanism*, expanding noticeably in the twentieth century, is virtually a religion and indeed most active. To include the Humanists is not unreasonable.

The religionists, you see, whatever their beliefs may be, make a practice of "lifting up their eyes unto the hills whence cometh their help." (We are indebted to King David for that lovely opening line from Psalm 121!)

In sharp contrast, the Humanists—the Atheists, Infidels, and Marxists—stand in front of a full-length mirror and examine their own image. Seriously they evaluate what they see. They never "lift up their eyes." "We are the highest and latest in the order of creation. We are the masters of our condition—for better or for worse. We need give no thanks to the causes and effects of an impersonal evolutionary process. We condemn ourselves for our failures, or we gaze into the mirror and say 'Well done!' "

Just completed is our survey of the activities of the European countries in taking over by conquest the lands and the people of the American continents and the continent of Africa. This took place, roughly speaking, between A.D. 1500 and 1900. What happened within

HINDUISM

AFGHANISTAN
O KABUL
PAKISTAN (WEST)
KASHMIR
AMRITSAR
PEOPLE'S REPUBLIC OF CHINA
TIBET
NEPAL
BHUTAN
ASSAM
KARACHI
DELHI
JAIPUR
INDIA
AGRA O
BENARES
CALCUTTA
BAN-GLA-DESH
BURMA
BOMBAY
MADRAS
FORMERLY EAST PAKISTAN
ARABIAN SEA
BANGLADORE
BAY OF BENGAL
CEYLON
(SRI LANKA)
1500 MILES

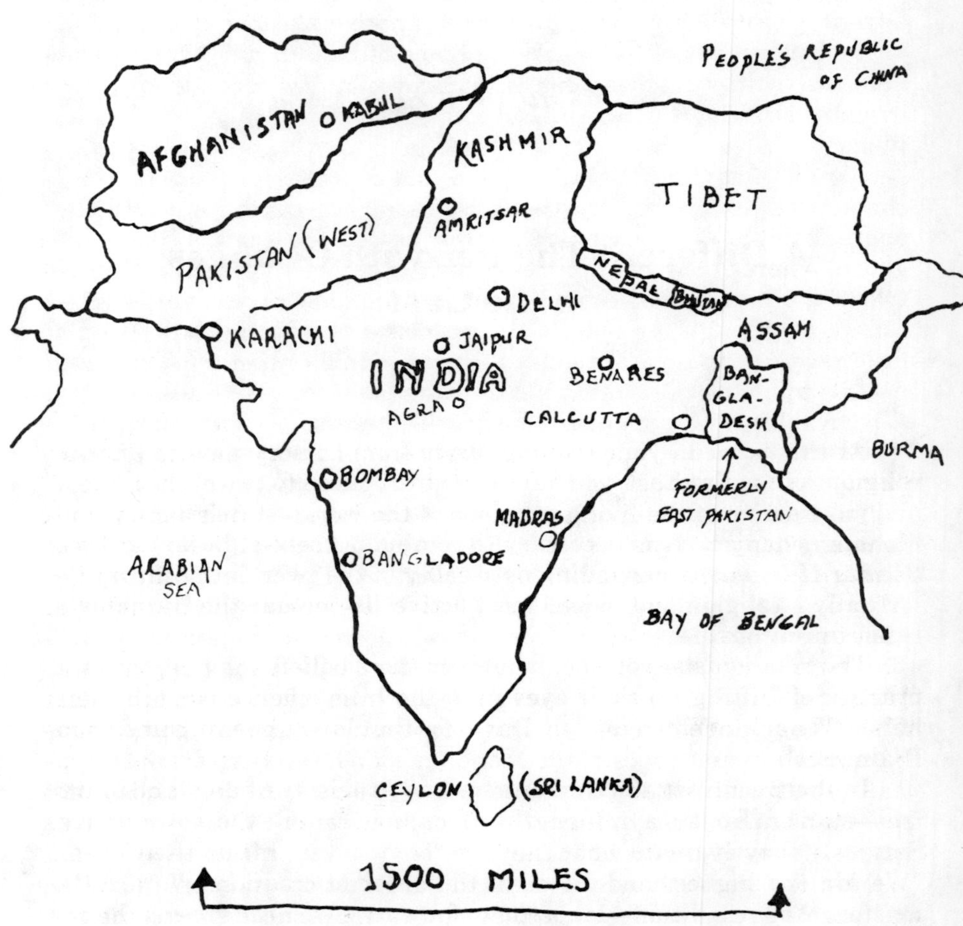

those 400 years is surely not novel in human history. Man has always been almost instinctively acquisitive in order to insure his survival. The most trivial invasion of a neighboring area not their own is a response to this urge. They want more of nature's abundance for their social group, whether in products or in living space. From the European adventure into Africa, we now turn to another theater of action—the vast subcontinent of India and the home of Hinduism. Later we shall note the further involvement of Mohammedanism, but we must first examine HINDUISM, a term that embraces both religious and political history.

To an "outsider," Hinduism is a complex, confusing, and seemingly chaotic religion. Even an exhaustive study can convey but a modest appreciation of its position and power among the world's living religions. Whereas our main purpose is to examine the relationship between the Indian peoples and their gods, or some Supreme Being, we cannot detach this study from the historical events that have been so fully recorded in several thousand years of India's history. The recent awards given to the motion picture *Gandhi* were well deserved. It is a biographical statement of the world-shaking accomplishments of Mahatma Gandhi. It makes real the fusion of religion and politics in human history.

If, in some moment of personal boredom, you should decide to seek meaning in such terms as TAGORE, PAKISTAN, JAIPUR, VISHNU, SARNATH, DHARMA, ARYAN, SHIVA, KARMA, BANGLADESH, AND SRI LANKA, you would find yourself launched into a bewildering assortment of beliefs, traditions, people, places, and political events. The more you can learn, the more rewarding will be your understanding and respect for a people whose passage from primitivism to nuclear fission boggles the mind. On that long road, the Indian people have both given to and opposed the Mohammedans, the British, the Christians, the Buddhists and the Zoroastrians. No other nation in the world reveals such a broad religious influence upon the daily lives of its people as one discovers in India.

Unlike most other religions, Hinduism claims no single founder. Its origins are so remote that they do not appear in recorded history. From where came all these people?

A reasonable theory is that the "Aryans," a people of common language and of primitive religious concepts, began a slow-moving migration from a point somewhere north of what we now name the Caspian Sea. The migration moved in several directions like the outstretched fingers of the open hand. Some went into Europe; some went east toward Mongolia. Those in whom we are now interested crossed the frontier of India and mingled with people already native to that region and of much darker skintone. Thus it is conjectured that Hindus are the result of that mixture. It was a land of physical magnificence, extending from the highest ranges of mountains in the world to the tropical beaches along the shores of the Indian Ocean. From this panoply of nature's abundance came the primitive worship of a variety of deities, specifically named and represented in thousands of man-made images. This idolatry exists today among the Indian people.

Somewhat like Christianity, but otherwise unrelated, Hinduism has created its own TRINITY of superhuman authority. By name they are called BRAHMA, The Creator, VISHNU, The Preserver, SHIVA, The Destroyer.

Beneath them, to serve human needs and desires, are countless lesser deities. They resemble the gods of the dead religions of the Babylonians, the Egyptians, the Semites, the Romans, the Greeks, the Mayas, the Incas, and the Aztecs.

But today, one discovers beneath this overwhelming display of gods, many well-educated, mystical Indians who speculate about one Universal Spirit. They tolerate but are totally indifferent to the gods of the masses. Mind you, all these people are Hindus. Their cohesiveness comes from something other than the plethora of gods. What is this "something"?

We find a portion of the answer when we consider three beliefs which are uniformly held by all:

Transmigration—When man dies, his soul returns to earth at some time in a new animation, not necessarily but probably as another human being either higher or lower in status than in the previous existence. This reincarnation will depend upon the quality of his earlier performance.

Dharma—Dharma is a collective term denoting all rites, ceremonies, and practices covering every aspect of life: marriage, eating, occupation, social intercourse, residence, business procedures, et cetera. The more carefully and faithfully a Hindu observes Dharma, the better will be the next life and the continuing existence of the soul.

Karma—Karma could be called the "machinery" of Dharma. It is the law of "cause and effect." The more conscientious one is in following Karma, the more rewarding will be the results of Transmigration and reincarnation.

The Caste System of Hinduism

Let's reflect for just a moment. A "classless society" has always been the dream of the idealist. What is a "classless society"? You are familiar with such groupings as "the workers' class," "the upper class," the "white-collar class," the "blue-collar class," the "professional class," the "lower class," and so on. They appear as descriptive terms every day in our newspapers and magazines.

There are two approaches in seeking a definition of the classless society: 1. It is a society in which there is an equitable distribution of all resources necessary for the maintenance of life among all mankind; and 2. It is a society that refuses to accept as criteria such discriminating categories as wealth, education, race, religion, personal achievement, social standing, and personality. It does not set up rigidly maintained groupings of people.

Worldwide, it is fair to say that the idealists have not had the satisfaction of creating a truly classless society. In our own democratic country, however, despite our retained prejudices and failures, it can also be said that no individual with determination and education can be held in a locked compartment of class discrimination. He may move up or down or remain within a group as he elects and as his endowed talents are progressively developed.

It is important to have these thoughts in mind when we consider India's caste system. There are four socio-religious castes in Hinduism:

The Brahmans—originally the priestly class; no longer so restrictive.
The Kshatryas—the ruling class; the ones in authority.
The Vaisyas—the business and merchant class;
The Sudras—the working class; the laborers.

Although these classes can be loosely described as professional or occupational, such description is today unreliable. One finds a kind of sectarianism even within separate castes. Some lines of demarcation are still retained; others have disappeared. Even so, these degrees of class differentiation make difficult the functioning of a democratic society.

Hinduism is therefore a "way of life" into which an individual is born—not admitted upon request. He is thus a birthright and lifelong member.

Neither are the beliefs of the people monitored by the priests, or as we say, "by the church." In Hinduism, a person may declare that he accepts none of the tenets of the religion and still remain a good Hindu, that is, so long as he is faithful in the observance of karma, dharma, and believes in transmigration.

Other beliefs held uniformly by Hindus are: 1. that woman is inferior to man; 2. that the cow is a sacred animal; and 3. that the material things of the world are without value.

Perhaps one can sum things up in this way—while recognizing the great number of highly educated Hindus and their participation in business, government, and world affairs, we note that people are under the influence of numerous superstitions. They live in fear of evil spirits and try to avoid their evil designs. To the tribesman of the forests and mountains, the god, or gods, not only eat and drink and sleep, but also have the power to bless or to curse. The gods exist on the sacrifices made to them.

The spirits of deceased ancestors may require food and water. The souls of the goats sacrificed to the goddess Kali are sure of a place in heaven. There seems to be no limit to the divinities that reside in animals, trees, rivers, and wells. These are powerful beliefs nurtured by the priestly class. Let it also be said, however, that portions of the sacred scriptures are as noble, as beautiful, and as supportive of the good life as one finds in the Judeo-Christian scriptures.

For further information about the dimensions of the religion of the Hindus, you should turn to investigative reading of your own. Talk it over with the school's librarian.

The Untouchables

There are some 60,000,000 Indians, however, who have not had the fortune of being born into a caste. They carry the name "Untouchables." For centuries, caste members who come into too close a relationship with an untouchable must follow a process of purification. This should not be thought of as a pattern of cruelty or social disdain. It is a requirement of an ancient religious mandate. It was against this discriminatory practice that Mahatma Gandhi, a Vaisya by birth, made a lifelong commitment (along with other prejudicial situations).

Within the twentieth century, much has happened to fracture, to moderate, and to weaken the monolithic caste system. Two world wars under the colonial administration of Great Britain, augmented by thousands of Americans and other nationalities, have exerted great pressure toward change. All these "outsiders," please note, were just as "untouchable" as were those of Indian origin. Then came the independence of India in 1947 and the establishment of a Federal Republic in 1950. India had already been admitted to the United Nations as a political entity under Britain in 1945.

Is Hinduism Really a Religion?

Most assuredly; Hinduism is a religion. The details of theological variations within this vast country are of relatively little importance so long as the foundational beliefs in transmigration, dharma, and karma are accepted. A Hindu is generally expected to respect and believe in the inspired scriptures of the *VEDA*—that Brahman priests are divinely appointed, and that the caste system is also of divine origin. Furthermore, against one's status in life there can be no rebellion, since one's lot is foreordained by birth.

There is evidence, however, that the caste system is beginning to fall apart. Laws to curb discriminatory practices have been put into effect. But it will be many years before noticeable change will come over the face of India. It is impossible to uproot in a few decades the traditions of several thousands of years.

As to acts of worship, although the country is literally crowded with temples to the various gods, Hinduism is not marked by scheduled attendance at worship services. The sacred books are not read to the people by the priests. Nor is any Hindu besides the priests expected to read them. Even if encouraged to do so, most of the masses cannot read. Statistics record a literacy of 36 percent.

Further Comments on India and Hinduism

One cannot fully comprehend the difficulties India has faced in taking her position among the nations of the modern world unless he looks into other conditions that India had to meet and control. This review is largely statistical.

Today's estimated population	700,000,000
Hindus number	550,000,000
Moslems number	80,000,000
Others	70,000,000

Beside the population problem, there is a languages barrier. Hindi, the language of Government is spoken by only 24 percent of the people—168,000,000.

Marathi, by	63,000,000	Rajasthani, by	32,900,000
Bengali, by	56,700,000	Urdu, by	31,500,000
Telegu, by	55,300,000	Punjabi, by	30,100,000
Tamil, by	53,000,000	Oriya, by	28,000,000
Kanarese, by	37,800,000	Malayali, by	27,300,000
Gujarati, by	34,300,000	Other languages	77,000,000

These figures do not include 75,000 Chinese, 120,000 Tibetans, and 150,000 Europeans.

During the years of British administration, the language of government was, understandably, English. The representatives from India's twenty-two states spoke English as a common language with the other members of parliament. With independence in 1947, however, there arose a demand that an Indian language be the language of parliament.

Because of the diversity of Indian languages, the arrival at an ultimate decision was preceded by revolts, rioting, and bloodshed. A compromise was eventually reached—Hindi and English would be associate languages in government.

Language, however, was but another of the seemingly insurmountable obstacles with which this incredible mixture of human beings had to contend. You have frequently heard the United States referred to as a gigantic "melting pot" of people and cultures because of immigration from all over the world by people seeking freedom or better living conditions. Although the American merger has been deeply troubled racially and even language-wise, we have come out with an end product that has demonstrated its unanimity in times of international conflict.

The trouble in India was that the "melting pot" of tribal languages and religions did not melt. Spread over the long territorial expanse from the Middle East to the steaming tropical jungles of Assam and Burma were the kingdoms and principalities of dozens of "royal" families protecting their much smaller holdings. Unity with others was not one of their priorities! The best publicized example of this was to be found among the Maharajahs. Their desire to retain their wealth and governing authority proved one of the greatest obstacles to national unification.

If this unification has been difficult in the twentieth century, what must it have been like 1200 years ago when the organized, sword carrying, and spiritually committed Mohammedans began their invasional thrusts eastward? In this abbreviated summary, we cannot go into the details of that conquest, but, considering the lack of today's modern mean of transportation and communication, the Islamic take-over of much of India dwarfs by comparison the European colonial occupation of Africa.

Turn back in the pages of this book to the map showing the expansion of the Mohammedan faith. Read the accompanying text. The magnitude of that Mohammedan occupation is quite convincing to modern travelers who marvel at the impressive architectural achievements of more than 300 years of Islamic domination (1526–1857). Whether this long series was carried out by Arabs, Persians, or Turks is immaterial to our present study. They were all followers of Mohammed, the one and only authentic prophet of their God, whose instructions were clearly set forth in the KORAN. Mosques, fortresses, burial tombs, and government buildings span a broad belt from Bombay to Calcutta. They make a significant contribution to KODAK! The tourist's knowledge of the KORAN is minimal!

Although the Islamic conquest of India can be described as territorial and economic expansionism, it was more truly a takeover by Koranic missionaries supported by the sword of their God. It contrasted totally with the missionary efforts of the earlier Christian disciples who proclaimed God's love for all people. To the Christian, acceptance of salvation was voluntary.

Upon Hinduism, the impact of this invasion was enormous. Many deserted the faith under compulsion. The very looseness of Hinduism's supervision of its followers made conformance to the new religion's demands relatively easy. But there was also violent resistance by certain groups as we shall later see.

That the resistance retained its vigor is shown in the twentieth century's partitioning of ancient India into East and West Pakistan. East Pakistan is now Bangladesh. The conflict between Hinduism and Mohammedanism still goes on. Religion and history do not walk hand-in-hand, but obviously we cannot comprehend either one without studying the other.

Perhaps we can best close this chapter by pointing out that the Indian people adhering to Hinduism are today free people under parliamentary government, thanks to the British influence. With a touch of irony, we can also say that all those people are brothers and sisters of about three and a half billion "Untouchables"! Within the past 400 years, long unmindful of the larger world, India has come into a relationship with the western world. By using a succession of vehicles of transport—camels, carts, donkeys, roads, trains, motorcars, and aeroplanes—they are now aware of nuclear energy and of the globe-circling Space Shuttle!

Chinese communism has now destroyed the earlier boundary lines with India by taking over Tibet. A violent world is no respecter of religious beliefs—especially a Communist world. Today, under the controversial leadership first of Prime Minister Indira Gandhi and now her son, India seeks industrial development and advancement in medicine, agriculture, and education. India owes much for the laying of good foundations in these areas to the years of British occupation. Another statistical presentation will indicate how great will be the struggle for success.

	India	United States
Area (sq. miles)	1,269,420	3,618,770
Population	700,000,000	230,000,000
Density of persons per sq. mile	551	64

If the governments of the world cannot do anything to promote population control, perhaps the world's religions will have to take over the task!

Ahead you will find an updated map showing the present placement of all significant world religions within the boundaries of India.

Suggested Subjects for Library Work and Reports

The Gods of India	The Hindu Trinity
Transmigration	Animal Sacrifice
Ancient *vs.* Modern	Sacred Rivers of India
The Caste System	The Untouchables
Tribal Religions in India	Moslem Architecture

You may find this hard to accept, but it will be no surprise at some later date to find a number of the students who are taking this course working in the research fields of archaeology and paleontology!

Chapter XI

Small but Important

The statistics on the preceding page may be so overpowering as to cause us to lose sight of the Jains, the Parsis, and the Sikhs—three religions of India with relatively small followings but of historical importance. Statistically, they look like this:

	Jains	**Parsis**	**Sikhs**
In India	3,200,000	115,000	13,886,000
Elsewhere	None	39,000	358,000

Sikhism

You will have noticed from the chart showing the lifelines of the world's religions that Sikhism is not an ancient religion. Guru Nanak, its founder, lived from 1469 to 1533. From the close of the fifteenth century down to India's independence from England in 1947, these doughty spiritual warriors were incredibly involved, both supportively and oppositionally, in episodes of violence that followed the Mohammedan and Christian invasions of India.

First, then, some facts about the Sikh's beliefs and practices:

1. Sikhism is the youngest of India's religions.
2. Nanak, the founder, came from the Jat race of northwest India.
3. Accepting the monotheistic concept of God, Nanak asserted that God was to be loved rather than feared.

India, the Melting Pot of Religions in Asia
(See key in lower left-hand corner)

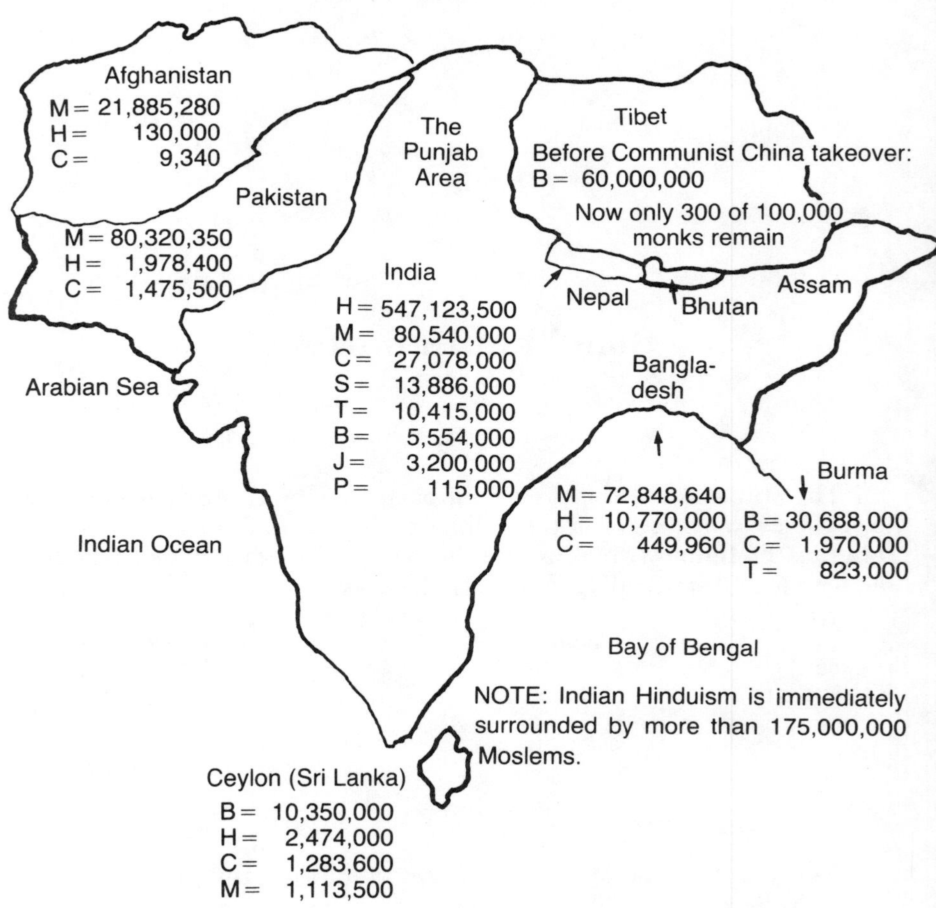

H = Hindus		547,123,500
M = Moslem		80,540,000
C = Christian		27,078,000
T = Tribal		10,415,000
S = Sikhs		13,886,000
B = Buddhists		5,554,000
J = Jains		3,200,000
P = Parsis		115,000

NOTE: All figures above and elsewhere in this book are taken from *The World Christian Encyclopedia*, Oxford University Press, 1982

4. He refused to accept the doctrine of transmigratiion, and he did not recognize as inspired either the Hindu scriptures or the Mohammedan Koran.
5. He opposed ascetic practices and professional religious begging. He encouraged his followers to lead active lives and permitted them to eat meat.
6. He opposed the caste system, teaching that all men are equal before God.
7. The term *Guru* is best translated as "master" or "Teacher." Guru Nanak was succeeded by nine other gurus. The line came to an end in 1708 with the death of the tenth guru, the famous Gobind Singh.
8. The writings of the gurus make up the scriptures of the Sikhs. The *Granth*, as the scriptures are called, is the equivalent for Sikhs of the Judeo-Christian Bible or of the Koran of Mohammedanism. By its teachings, the Sikhs have directed their lives since the death of the last guru.
9. Under the later gurus, the Sikhs became a self-ordained nation as well as a religious order and carved out for their homeland that portion of northwest India that is marked on the map as the Punjab area.
10. The professed objective of the Sikhs was to restore harmony between the feuding Mohammedans and Hindus. Instead, they soon found themselves at war with the Moslems. They have remained bitter opponents of Islam ever since. Their relations with the Hindus have been much better, although much fractured by the recent assassination of Prime Minister Indira Gandhi.
11. Often during British occupation, they fought the British. Later, however, they became staunch allies. The Sikhs have long been a familiar sight to travelers in the various outposts of British colonialism. Their turbaned headdress and erect bearing were impressive in Singapore, Shanghai, and Hong Kong before World War II.
12. Contemporary Sikhism reveals the presence of Hindu, Mohammedan, and Christian influences; some outside observers believe that Sikhism will eventually be reabsorbed into Hinduism. Karma and dharma are already creeping back. The Sikhs are a proud people, however, and this pride may help to retain their religious identity even though most of the Sikhs do not even read the Granth. which at one time was published in six languages.

JAINISM
SIKHISM
PARSIISM
AFGHANISTAN
KABUL
(CHINA)
TIBET
PAKISTAN
NEPAL
BHUTAN
DELHI
KARACHI
JAIPUR
BENARES
INDIA
BANGLA DESH
AGRA
CALCUTTA
BURMA
ARABIAN SEA
BOMBAY
MADRAS
BAY OF BENGAL
INDIAN OCEAN
SRI LANKA (CEYLON)
AMRITSAR
1500 MILES

Considering the violence that followed the British partitioning of India into West Pakistan, India, and East Pakistan upon granting independence in 1947–50, the marvel is that the Sikhs continue to dominate the Punjab area where their historic capital, Amritsar, is the destination of thousands of today's tourists (see map). The recent tragic hostilities have shocked an unbelieving world.

After partition, the war between India and Pakistan (1971) resulted in an Indian victory. East Pakistan was eliminated as a part of Pakistan and became known as Bangladesh, a Moslem nation. Some ten millions of Hindus fled back to the mother country when the war began and later. Now independent and a member of the United Nations, Bangladesh is under military rule just as are so many of the newly freed colonies in Africa.

It is noted that both India and Bangladesh have signed suppportive agreements with Moscow. Our own relationship with India is at the moment one of poor quality because of our support of Pakistan since its separation from India. Once more we are aware that political changes are inseparable from religious prejudices.

Suggestion:

To provide relief from the monotony of this outline of religious history, drop in at your school library and ask for *The World's Great Religions*, published by TIME INC. (LIFE) in 1957. Although that publication does not give the Jains, Sikhs, and Parsis great religious status, the opening chapter provides, with superb color illustrations, a splendid augmentation of what you have just been reading.

The Parsis

Parsiism is not a religion of Indian origin. The Parsis were Persians, last referred to in this book when covering the problems of the Jewish people in the fifth and sixth centuries B.C. They might indeed be referred to as some of the earliest refugees from political and religious persecution. Although they played their part in the destruction of the Jewish nation of Israel and Judah, their turn came also to be in deep trouble. Their later refugee status is directly assignable to followers of Mohammed. Some of these Persians, unwilling to respond to Islam's sword-backed demands for surrender, fled eastward and came to reside in western India. In the Bombay area are to be found most of 115,000 Parsis who survive. They had abandoned their homeland, which is now largely within the boundaries of Iran.

Their somewhat legendary founder was named Zarathrushtra or Zoroaster. Popularly they are referred to as Zoroastrians. Zarathrushtra was a deeply religious leader whose theology offered a continuing battle between Truth and Evil. The sun was the symbol of total truth, and the followers were called sun-worshipers.

Highly educated by comparative Indian standards, the Parsis are today the financiers and industrialists of India. They are in no way to be associated with the caste system, but they are a proud group and are in a social grouping as elite as the Brahmans.

That Zoroaster was a great religious leader cannot be denied. Had he been followed by others as great (as was true of the Jewish people), the religion might have attained similar prominence. One of their practices to which attention is most frequently called has to do with the disposal of the dead. To the Parsis earth, water, and fire are sacred and pure. The deceased is impure. Therefore they neither bury the dead nor burn the remains as do the Hindus. The bodies are placed within small enclosures, looking something like a small, rounded arena. Almost immediately, the large vultures of India drop from their expectant perches along the top of the wall and very quickly reduce the body to skeletal condition. It can now be buried without contaminating the earth. These places are called "Towers of Silence." Of course, no spectators are ever admitted, even to their regular temples of worship. How different this is from the cremation of Gandhi following his assassination in 1948. The witnessing crowds were tremendous.

The Parsis, like all other religions, have their scriptural writings. The title of the main body is the *Zendavesta*. There are also the writings of Zoroaster himself. If you're interested, you can read these in English translation. They read much like some of the passages of the Old Testament.

As is also true of most religions, the Parsis have sectarian disagreement. The modernists are crying for reform, and the old orthodox Parsis wish to retain the customs and ritualisms of the past. It is a stern religion with a high ethical code. Tourists who today have opportunity to meet with Parsis are impressed by their handsomeness and the influence they exert on the Indian economy. Another distinguishing feature is that they require no veiling or concealment of the faces of women—so common in Hindu and Mohammedan cultures.

The Jains

For a change of pace, let us imagine that a dedicated Jain is making an informative statement of his beliefs to a group of non-Jains. Hear him:

"Good friends, I am indeed fortunate to have this opportunity to address you. I am but one of many who bless this country of India as our home. I speak of course, in Gujarati, not Hindi. In India you surely must know, we have fourteen distinct different languages, and communication is often very difficult. Even within our own religion we have trouble. Many of the followers of the great Mahavira, our founder, speak Rajasthani.

"We are fairly well concentrated in north central India, with active centers in Delhi and Jaipur. You can find these cities on the map which I have included.

"I should say that there is much about Hinduism that still guides our lives, but we have abandoned our belief in transmigration. We still hold on to dharma and to karma. Our commonly shared, profound belief is that man must so conduct his life here on earth that he can escape the cycle of rebirth. He enters a subliminal peace forever—a spirit separated from the human body. The vast number of the gods of Hinduism have no meaning to us at all. Neither do we depend upon a Supreme Being for a final reward for excellence, like the adherents of Christianity, Mohammedanism, and Judaism. We achieve this noble estate by our own strivings toward purity of soul.

"Our religion is often reported as being a subsidiary of Buddhism. That is not exactly true. There is a similarity between the Buddhist Nirvana and our own final peace for the human spirit, but there are other differences that separate us. The best description is to be found in our published scripture entitled Ahimsa. This calls for an all-inclusive respect for all forms of life. For instance, we carry our belief to the end that we love even the tiny ants that cross our pathway, and we carefully sweep the ground or the pavement before us lest we inadvertently step upon one of these creatures. The most difficult profession for us to undertake, however, is farming. This requires the turning over of the soil in which many of nature's little spirits abide. So we usually leave that occupation to others. We are much better off in the field of handling money and running businesses where temptation to be creature-careful seldom presents itself.

"A further restriction causes more difficulty. We do not permit the remarriage of widows. This works against the growth of our religious following. There is already substantial evidence that we are not keeping pace with other religions. One result of this practice is that many of our friends become monks. Some go so far as to reject clothing and walk about on their little pilgrimages stark naked. I personally do not agree with this and belong to the white-robe constituency as you can see.

"The pursuit of eternal peace must recognize the fallibility of man. Some detour on byroads of compromise. Keepers of the faith recognize that this is true of all religions.

"It has been pleasant talking with you, and I hope that when we next come together some others of us from different faiths will be as frank as I have been about my own."

Well that is a fair presentation of this extraordinary body of worshipers. What he has told us does reveal that the Jains approach quite closely the Buddhists. Both can be regarded as separatists from Hinduism.

As the written records report, Mahavira, the founder, came from a background of luxurious contentment. He was denied nothing that could please his senses. Troubled by this freedom, he took on the life of an ascetic, denying all physical longings. Thus would he escape the cycle of rebirth. Today, as happens so often, the founder of the Jain faith has been given almost the stature of a god. He and some twenty-four of his successors, called Tirthankaras, are worshiped in the Jain temples. They seem to function as a sort of Committee of Gods rather than as a Supreme Being. The Jains would be prompt to assert that they are not Atheists.

Some of the selections from the Jain scriptures, the *Agamas*, will give you by translation some ideas of the austerity of the lives of the followers of Mahavira.

> . . . He should not be attached to transitory pleasures. . . . He should not nourish desire or greed. He should be enlightened by eternal objects and not trust in the elusive power of the many gods. . . .
>
> He is careful in his walk . . . lest he might with his feet hurt or displace or injure or kill living beings. . . .
>
> He does not regard or contemplate the lovely forms of women; does not recall to his mind the pleasures and amusements he formerly had with women. He does not drink too much, nor does he drink liquors or eat highly seasoned dishes.
>
> He renounces all attachments, whether little or much, small or great, living or lifeless. Neither shall he form such attachments or cause others to do so. . . . As long as he lives, he shall confess

and blame, repent and exempt himself from those sins . . . in speech and mind and body.

Well, when one hears of the restrictions laid upon the followers of Mahavira and his successors, he is not surprised at the slow growth in the number of Jains. He can see why Jains are beginning to return to the less exacting demands of Hinduism.

Suggested Theme Topics:
The Parsi "Towers of Silence"
The Sikh-Moslem Relationship
Religious Codes *versus* Individual Freedom
The Great Gobind Singh
British-Sikh Relations
Moslem-Hindu Conflict in India
Sacrifice—Its Purpose and Practice

God in the Rain

Upward I went to the mountain's top
To talk with God who leaned down
From a gray cloud
And cooled my face.

The years of life stared up at me
Along the rugged slopes.
The wrenching sorrows of the past
And all my failures lay below me.
I wept no longer.

Here, with wet wind blowing on my face,
I felt the presence and the comfort
Of my God who stooped from out
The leaden skies and spoke inaudibly
And yet resoundingly of Faith.

Gratefully, with singing heart,
I started on my downward way.
The quiet voice walked with me.
"You should ascend this mountain every day!"

L.R.S. (1925)

Chapter XII

A Pause to Remember

Let us take time now to review what we have so far covered in our desire to emphasize the inseparability of history and religion when presenting the story of man's development through the passage of time—a passage that we conveniently arrange in a succession of days, weeks, months, years, and centuries.

We have paid tribute to the intelligence displayed in the functioning of the human brain, an organ of man's physical body. We have noted the brain's centrality in directing the responses of other parts of the body through a network of message-carrying nerves.

Amazingly, given proper nourishment through a complex of supporting organs, man continues to walk about in his environment within a segment of time of which the precise duration is not predictable. Then the physical body dies, and the elements that nourished its former existence revert to an inert state, where they keep silent company with formerly active creatures. All such creatures, man has reasonably placed in a category labeled "The Animal Kingdom." This is distinct from two other categories— "The Vegetable Kingdom" and "The Mineral Kingdom."

Throughout time's passage, man, whom we have chosen to designate as a human being, has outrun his (we dare say) competitors of the Animal Kingdom. True, like the human being, they experience hunger, react instinctively to pain, heat, sound, and sight, and respond periodically to reproductive stimuli. At no time, however, do such creatures assemble in meeting to examine the human being's success in dominating the Animal Kingdom. Even the most highly developed of species do little beyond eating, drinking, sleeping, mating, and swinging aloft among the branches of the trees in their habitat. They identify their enemies and instinctively protect those whom they recognize as "family."

The human being, however, early recognized in himself a stage of development that surpassed that of his earthly companions of forest, field, and stream. Many years ago, he began the practice of meeting in small groups to pass collective judgments upon thoughts held as individuals. Out of this community of thinkers poured a succession of established facts and theories of probability for ideas lacking proof. That they were here on solid, comforting ground they doubted not. Nor did they doubt that others much like themselves had preceded them. They discovered a legacy of written symbols which could be translated into a spoken language, in purpose like their own.

Their little discussion groups increased in size. They spoke to one another in Greek, Persian, Latin, Hindi, Mandarin, and later in English, French, Italian, Spanish, German, and Swedish. They published their monographs, quarterly journals, newspapers, periodicals, and gave visible reports in sound and full color on television.

Electronically, they hurled messages at satellites 22,000 miles above the earth and retrieved them thousands of miles distant in split seconds. They walked and drove upon the surface of the moon, circled the earth in space shuttles, and got daily reports as to what was happening in the vaporous reaches of the cosmos.

As to the human body? That was indeed ancient history. The functions of the heart, the kidneys, the salivary glands, the bloodstream, and a hundred other units of the physiological machinery were common knowledge in thousands of centers of medical learning and practice. Only a few troublesome questions remained to be answered: How and when did this remarkable progression originate? What was there before there was anything? How can man account for the gap of information about and between those that swing in the trees and those who have built their temples out of the Cedars of Lebanon?

Well, the human being was not about to anaesthetize that remarkable brain. He would continue to look for answers. Donning his hiking shoes and attaching a compass, altimeter, and fathometer to his blue jeans, he set out. With him he carried a pick, a shovel, and a soft-haired brush. His questing mind rejoiced upon discovering the skeletal remains of an enormous reptile. Carefully he dusted the fragile image of a tree fern. Diving into the ocean's depths, he located the trail that led from fin to feather. Back in the laboratory, he made a fascinating chart that led continuously from the amoeba and atom to the swinger of the tree tops.

The day was late. Closing the laboratory door, the human being made for home where spouse greeted spouse and children with "I love you! It's good to be home again."

We honor our scientists, are proud of their achievements, and are grateful for the evidence they have produced in support of the evolutionary theory that had been so much advanced by a long delayed report of the timid young Englishman, Charles Darwin, nearly 150 years ago. He feared the opposition that the theory might generate among others who held a quite different theory.

We can best approach an understanding of this second theory by offering volumes of historical facts that have been collected by the laboratory scientists whom we have just applauded. Through the skills of anthropologists, archaeologists, and social philosophers, we have been given a brilliant picture of the human being's continuous search for a relationship with a Supreme Being whose power and authority rule the destinies of both individuals and groups.

From their collective reports, we note the bronzed, stalwart figure, spear in hand, who stands on a rocky ledge overlooking a broad expanse of tropical verdure. Far away, from the cone of a volcano pours a river of molten gold. Clustered about a charcoal fire before the cave entrance are children and a woman with pendant breasts. Their faces reflect concern as they feel the ledge beneath their broad, flat feet gently vibrate. Ceremoniously, all kneel before the grotesque image carved from the stalk of a giant tree fern. Upon its foreshortened torso they drape a circlet of hibiscus blossoms.

The worshipers are obviously human beings—provably so. They are very much like us who sit in Room 204 looking at the color reproductions of Mount St. Helens in the *National Geographic*. Far below the ridge, the tree swingers leap from branch to branch and vine to vine beneath the forest canopy.

We turn the pages of the latest quarterly journal of scientific discovery; or, if cost is no obstacle, of the 11" × 14" cumbersome volume ($53.74). What a story it offers! A true story! The bronzed spear-holding human has passed a torch from his charcoal fire to the children and grandchildren. It's like watching a gigantic Olympiad. Its light spreads from valley to valley, crosses ranges of mountains and the searing deserts of the drifting continents of the earth. It illuminates the entrance to the Pyramid's sarcophagi, lights the joss sticks in the bronze urn below Kwan Yin, and intensifies the lustre of the golden doors of the Ark of the Covenant.

Tirelessly, ever onward, the torchbearers pass the flame. Held aloft in the gnarled hands of fishermen from Galilee, it lights the shores of the Mediterranean Sea. A diversionary flame enhances the faces of the pilgrims in the Kaaba at Mecca. On again to St. Peter's in Rome, to Notre Dame, to Chartres, Exeter, Salisbury, Winchester, and Canterbury. The shadows of soaring Gothic columns give way before the insistent flame. The choral voices of thousands of human beings rise to the heavens in both praise and supplication.

Undaunted by the rough seas and the roaring winds, another band of pilgrims, sheltering the flame, step upon the rocky shore at Plymouth and kneel in thanksgiving.

The years pass swiftly. Fifty-six human beings assemble in Independence Hall in Philadelphia. Brightly, unwaveringly, the torch iluminates the document to which they append their names: "For the support of this declaration, with a firm reliance on the Protection of Divine Providence, we mutually pledge to each other our lives, our fortunes, and our sacred Honor."

***

We close the cumbersome book with its fascinating illustrations. What a marvelous accounting! Yes, these are the facts of history—not a theory. We are indeed indebted to our researchers of laboratory, field, and stream. They have accumulated the evidence to show, beyond the shadow of a doubt, that the human being, quite apart from the tree swingers, has been "lifting his eyes" from prehistoric time to the elevation of the Host by the archbishop in his ornamented vestments.

From this spiritual urge has come the second theory—totally unscientific—that God, however He may be described in the cultures of the world, is responsible for the wonders of Creation. We look upon a different evolutionary movement. It is unsupported by microscope, centrifuge, pick and shovel, or spectrometer. It is a theory underwritten by FAITH, which functions intuitively, much as the baby chimpanzee identifies its mother. There the similarity ends. Periodically, small "strikes" take place among the disparate body of worshipers, but the mainstream continues to flow, unbroken. A popular exponent of the theory puts it much more gracefully: "FAITH is the substance of things hoped for; the evidence of things not seen."

Let us indulge in another fantasy. Just summoned into meeting by the United Nations is the First Ecumenical Congress. Gathered under the flags of many nations, the delegates jostle for position under the appeals of the cameraman charged with recording the event. For one brief moment the group stands motionless.

"Splendid!" shouts the photographer. "Now will you all please smile and hold hands?"

128

We have never received a copy of that negative, but we do recall some of the faces: Abraham, Moses, Elijah, Mohammed, Mahavira, Gautama Buddha, Zoroaster, Mohandas Gandhi, Wesley, Luther, King David, Calvin, the bishop of Rome, Washington Carver, and Florence Nightingale. And seated center, in the place of honor reserved for the Chairman of the Congress, is the bronzed, stalwart figure of a human being with spear in one hand and a wreath of hibiscus blossoms extended by the other.

***

Now then! In a very real way, this is what this course is about. From what we have been over thus far, we do not find these delegates holding hands and smiling. In Central America and the Middle East they are killing one another. They are dying violently in Iran, Iraq, Chad, and Afghanistan. Sikhs are murdering Hindus in the Punjab, and the anti-religionists are sending Christians into enslavement in Siberia.

And what about us here in our beloved country? The illuminated document announced our FAITH in Providence, and the Constitution assured all comers—Jews, Mohammedans, Buddhists, Hindus, Tribalists, and nonbelievers—that all were welcome to live among us, free from government interference in the practice of their faiths. That is the Christian approach. We have no Church of State to enforce it. We the people, have done this! By our actions of more than 200 years we implement a nonscientific theory. Somehow it seems just right that we should tell you again about the vision of the Founding Fathers who passed on to you the torch which, they say, lights the way from Alpha to Omega.

129

Full Cycle

On some clear night, when the full moon
Is white above the trees, the air bites sharply,
And the mist arises from the long wet grasses,
The frost will come.

Behold the change! The dull greens
Of late September will, by God's magic,
Become October's gaiety.
The hills will blush with red and gold—
With yellow and with purple.
The vines and berry bushes, a crimson tangle.
The evergreens alone look down
In solemn dignity upon the yearlings'
Final joyous fling.

If you return two weeks from now,
The colors will have passed
Into their crinkly browns, and every breeze
Will waft the sleeping leaves
To the frosted, drooping grasses
Upon the earth beneath.
Sleep well! Sleep well
Until your children hear
Heaven's call and rise to April sun—
The cyclic mission done.

L.R.S.
1924

Chaper XIII

We Move to the Far East

So far you have learned of two dispersal points for the two great missionary religions of the world—Christianity and Mohammedanism: 1. Jerusalem and its environs where Christianity began its world-embracing journey as the beneficiary of Jewish montheism; 2. Mecca, in Saudi Arabia, from which Mohammed (A.D. 570–632) launched his armed forces both east and west, carrying the word of God as updated through special and final revelation to Mohammed.

Following the breakup of great King David's Jewish nation and the later crucifixion of Jesus, Christianity turned its attention to the surrounding strongholds of Paganism. After six centuries of agonizing progress, the "Cross" was widely distributed along the Mediterranean shores and northward into Europe.

Suddenly appeared the new competitor—Mohammedanism. Like contestants in boxing, they smote one another for some 800 years, including the 200 years of the Crusades and the final retreat of the Moslems from southwestern Europe. By A.D. 1500, the public's judgment acknowledged Christianity's firm hold on Europe and Islam's prevailing influence over the entire Middle East and North Africa. Christianity retained but a small area of influence in the Near East, its point of origin.

During a long intermission (A.D. 1500–1800), Europe, largely Christian, headed west on "The Atlantic Navigation Freeway" and soon took over the North, Central, and South American homelands of the fading Indian cultures. They had also been successful in colonizing all of Africa despite the residual Islamic influence.

While Europe's Christians were accomplishing these ends, the Mohammedans were not just sitting on their hands in Mecca! They took off to the east, where the thrust of the Christians had been only spasmodic. Soon all of the Middle East and most of India were under their control, along with portions of north China, southeast Asia, and Indonesia.

Meanwhile, the Christian nations of Europe, with the Americas well in hand or in prospect, turned their attention also to the Far East. They would soon be giving the people from Mecca aggressive competition. Of course, Spain and Portugal had been out there since the sixteenth century. Spain had reached the "savages" of the Philippines. Portugal took over the island of Timor and kept active two trading posts: Goa on the west coast of India and Macao, near Hong Kong, in China. They still hold Macao.

By 1884, France had occupied what is now Vietnam and many islands of the South Pacific. The Dutch had moved in on much of Indonesia in 1800. Then England gained control of India and added Burma as a part of "British India." That was in the 1850s. For good measure, the British added Singapore, Malaysia, and Hong Kong, the counterimage of Macao. Only Thailand (Siam) managed to retain its monarchical little empire. Farther north, the stolid dynasties of China looked impassively down on all the commotion.

It is essential that we have in mind this progression of events as we turn to the study of Buddhism. Originating in India about 500 B.C. as an offshoot of the older Hinduism, it was about to leap over the high Himalayas, not on quest for territory or governing authority, but with missionary fervor. Today Buddhism is to be found in volume *outside* India. China, all countries of southeast Asia, Korea, the Indonesian chain, and the islands of the South Pacific are areas of great concentration. Japan should also be included, although the Buddhist influence there has been greatly diluted. You have already observed when we were considering the American continents how far afield many of the Buddhists have wandered.

If we accept Jerusalem and Mecca as the religious dispersal centers of the Middle East, then we must reasonably accept India as the one other great dispersal center in the Far East. Long before the Sikhs, the Jains, and the Parsis were religious facts, a handsome young Indian of the Kshatrya caste had been born into financial security, had been given the best education available, and was married to a princess who bore him a son, Rahula. This young man was Siddartha Gautama. The site was the small kingdom of Nepal in northeast India. What more could a young man want?

Instead, Gautama turned from the sensuous life to seek spiritual contentment. He renounced royal surroundings and riches. He walked forth from the palace, perhaps taking a final look at his princess wife and son. At age twenty-nine he became a homeless wanderer in search of salvation. For the next six years he wandered over the hillsides and valleys at the base of the magnificent snow-covered Himalayas. On clear days he could see Mount Everest. He talked with hermits and ascetics, hoping to discover what they had learned about life that might help him solve his own problems. They had very little to offer that he had not already learned for himself. He subjected his body to stress and mortification, denying himself proper sustenance. He still could find no inner peace.

Then one day, at age thirty-five, he sat down to meditate under the inviting shade of a huge tree. With suddenness, the "Enlightenment" came. The road to the eternal survival of his spirit in Nirvana lay quite simply revealed in the appropriate life-style. This is what he discovered, much as Mohammed would learn the "final truth" from the Angel Gabriel. And here follows what the Buddha learned at the time of his discovery:

The Four Noble Truths

1. All existence involves suffering;
2. Suffering is caused by man's earthly desires;
3. Suffering can be banished by eliminating desires;
4. The "Eight-Fold Path" tells one how to do this:

   a. Right thinking,
   b. Right aspirations—charity, pity, brotherhood,
   c. Right speech,
   d. Right conduct,
   e. Right livelihood—not harming others,
   f. Right mental effort,
   g. Right attention-alertness,
   h. Right meditation.

All this information came to the Buddha while meditating under the Bodhi Tree (ficus religiosa), as the flora people identify it. For the next forty-five years, he traveled the length and breadth of northern India, building a discipleship on the basis of doing away with all worldly desires. The Hinduism from which his caste forebears had sprung lost all appeal. He would have no need for idols, for sacrifices, or for a priesthood to revere the many gods and give instruction to the masses. The gloomy prospect of transmigration's handout was eliminated. His spirit would float free forever in a state called Nirvana—the elysian fields of foreverness. Man must provide his own spiritual salvation.

At this point, I pause for another interlude. Through the years I have developed an avocational interest in the birds, the bees, and the trees. Nature was a bountiful teacher. Recently my wife and I dropped in to a chain restaurant on U.S. Route 1 in South Miami, Florida. We enjoyed a repast of fried clams, bought a half-gallon container of ice cream, and walked out to our car, parked in an open space under towering trees. As I inserted the key in the door lock, my attention was caught by the long, heart-shaped, pointed leaves above my head. Yes, there could be no doubt! The single leaf which I had picked from an overhanging branch had come from *ficus religiosa*, a descendant of the Bodhi tree of northern India. What a coincidence that we should be standing under that tree, holding a carton of ice cream as I recalled Buddha's enlightenment!

And one more such true account, without your permission! It was in 1927, a long time ago, that this same couple stood on a crumbling wall that outlined the deer park in Sarnath, a short distance from Benares, a most sacred city of India. Across an open, weed-grown expanse we saw the ruins of what at one time had served as a monastery in Sarnath. It had been there that Buddha had preached his first sermon after his discovery of the Four Noble Truths under the Bodhi tree. We were returning to America after five years of work in China. In our informal studies, Sarnath had taken on deep meaning. As we stepped from the low wall, some stone rubble rolled down into the grasses. Abruptly we stopped as a glistening cobra glided silently away—the same specie that we had seen so often reproduced in the intricate carvings of the temples throughout Asia.

The outstanding characteristic of Buddhism has been its adaptability to whatever conditions it might encounter on its journeys. Buddhism was headed for China! Of course, that was long after Buddha's death. There had been caravan routes between China and India for several hundred years before Christ.

The process of Buddhism's establishment in China was slow. The Chinese had already developed a high order of civilization and culture. They looked with suspicion at invaders from across the borders. In the centuries that followed, Buddhism went through several periods of persecution. The worst of these occurred in A.D. 845, when Emperor

Wu Tsung, a Taoist by religious leaning, ordered the destruction of over 4000 Buddhist monasteries and 40,000 temples. Some 260,000 monks and nuns were compelled to return to secular life. The great accumulations of literature were burned. (It occurs to one that that tragedy closely resembles the action of Mao Tze-tung's Red Guards who were turned loose on the accumulation of foreign "gifts" during the Cultural Revolution of 1966–1976.)

Chinese Buddhism never fully recovered from this blow, even though the emperor's decree was rescinded two years later when he fell ill. We can be sure that Siddartha Gautama would never have sanctioned the variety of rituals, customs, and the priesthood that had been developed in his name.

As Buddhism mingled with Taoism—more about that later—it took into its religious household many gods which had no good reason to be there. The same procedure took place subsequently in Korea and Japan—and about that, more later. The end result has been the development of many sects. Most of the teachings have nothing to do with the stern tenets of the founder. The practices that are today closest to the original enlightenment of Buddha are to be found in Sri Lanka (Ceylon) in what is called southern Buddhism—the Mahayana Buddhism of scriptural writing—quite different from the northern Hinayana Buddhism.

In these late years of the twentieth century, Buddhism is experiencing a modest revival. The saffron-robed, shaven-headed youths who solicit your gifts in our airports belong to Buddhist sects. In Honolulu, a Buddhist temple now operates a "Sunday School" for the children. Occasionally, one can discover a relationship to the earlier Hinduism in the powerful concepts of transmigration and dharma.

Great and good as Buddhism has been for centuries, it seems to have lost its dynamism. Today, where the ancient temples are being restored in all their pristine beauty, the act seems to be a cultural salvation rather than a solace to the concerned and worried people who enter to light their tapers before the countless statues that look back silently at the supplicants. Furthermore, more than thirty years of communism in China have done much to stamp out or to hamper religious practice, whatever the faith of the believer. In my own recent trips to the Far East, I note with some feeling of delight, that people are still turning to religion. Even the young are in the temples and churches of the land whenever the doors may be safely opened by government grant.

I confess frustration at having to rush through something so significant in man's history as we are here doing. In justification, I can only say that the purpose of this book is NOT to arraign in figurative battle-order the oppositional forces of theological beliefs, ritualistic practices, with their Davids and Goliaths. It is to invite the reader to examine more carefully that compulsion of human beings to discover a faith, durable and unshakable, which can give meaning to life.

The Religions of the Far East

	Buddhist	Christian	Moslem	Hindu	Population
Bangladesh	530,000	449,960	72,848,640	10,770,000	84,803,000
Burma	30,688,000	1,970,900	1,268,000	310,000	35,195,000
China	53,391,000	1,800,000	21,356,760	0	889,865,000
Taiwan	7,492,000	1,288,140	84,500	0	17,423,000
India	5,554,000	27,078,000	80,540,000	547,123,500	694,309,000
Indonesia	1,500,000	17,069,900	67,213,000	3,250,000	154,869,000
Japan	70,011,240	3,526,000	0	0	117,546,000
Kampuchea	8,316,900	56,000	225,800	0	9,409,000
Korea N.	300,000	161,900	0	0	17,926,000
Korea S.	5,804,000	11,409,800	3,700	0	37,444,000
Laos	2,150,350	67,000	37,000	0	3,721,999
Malaysia	890,000	861,000	6,923,000	1,035,800	13,998,000
Mongolia	36,500	3,300	26,200	0	1,869,000
Singapore	209,600	208,630	424,000	138,900	2,437,000
Thailand	45,562,530	521,400	1,930,000	83,000	49,473,000
Vietnam	26,890,000	3,627,000	486,000	0	48,634,000
	253,772,120	43,020,930	172,826,600	562,711,200	1,484,616,000
	17%	2.8%	11.6%	38%	70%

Since these four religions constitute 70 percent of the total population, then 30 percent are tribalists, shamanists, spiritists, atheists, nonreligious, et cetera. Also omitted are Confucianists, Taoists, and Shintoists.

Points to Notice

1. Christians rank lowest in number.
2. Christians rank second in Indonesia.
3. There are more Christians than Buddhists in India.

Percentage by Countries

	Buddhists	Christian	Moslems	Hindus	Others
Bangladesh	6/10%	5/10%	86%	12.7%	2/10%
Burma	87%	5.5%	3.6%	8/10%	3.1%
China	6%	2/10%	2.4%	0	91.4%
Taiwan	43%	7. %	4/10%	0	49.6%
India	8/10%	3.9%	11.6%	78.8%	4.9%
Indonesia	9/10%	11%	43.3%	2%	42.7%
Japan	59.5%	2.9%	0	0	37.6%
Kampuchea	88.3%	6/10%	2.4%	0	8.7%
Korea N.	1.6%	9/10%	0	0	97.5%
Korea S.	15.5%	30.4%	9/100%	0	54%
Laos	5.7%	1.8%	9/10%	0	91.6%
Malaysia	6.4%	6.1%	49.5%	7.4%	10.6%
Mongolia	1.9%	1/10%	1.4%	0	96.6%
Singapore	8.6%	8.5%	17.4%	5.6%	59.9%
Thailand	92%	1%	3.9%	2/10%	3%
Vietnam	55.2%	7.4%	9/10%	0	36.5%

We should not leave Buddhism without noticing its rapid entrance into Korea. By A.D. 372, the monks from China had won favor with the ruling dynasty of Korea. It spread rapidly among a people less advanced than the Chinese. From Korea to Japan later, as we shall see.

The importance of this map is that it shows the remarkable shift in religious interest since those early days.

North Korea (Communist)

Buddhists 300,000
Christians   161,900
Others (?) 17,926,000

Christians and Buddhists make up only 2½% of the population.

South Korea

Christians 11,409,000
Buddhists 5,804,000
Others..20,231,000

Christians and Buddhists make up 46% of the total population.

It was the Buddhist scholars who brought the first written language to both Korea and Japan. The written language was CHINESE!

U.S.S.R
BUDDHISM
1985
OUTER MONGOLIA
INNER MONGOLIA
36,500
70,000,000
JAPAN
300,000
N.
KOREA
S.
5,800,000
PEKING
LOYANG
YELLOW SEA
PEOPLE'S REPUBLIC OF CHINA
SHANGHAI
TIBET
NEPAL
BHUTAN
SARNATH
BENARES
5,554,000
CALCUTTA
INDIA
53,392,000
HONGKONG
CANTON
7,442,000
TAIWAN
BURMA
30,688,000
BAY OF BENGAL
THAILAND
45,562,000
VIETNAM
26,088,000
PHILIPPINES
34,000
MALAYSIA
899,000
CEYLON
SINGAPORE
210,000
BORNEO
CELEBES
INDONESIA
1,500,000
AUSTRALIA

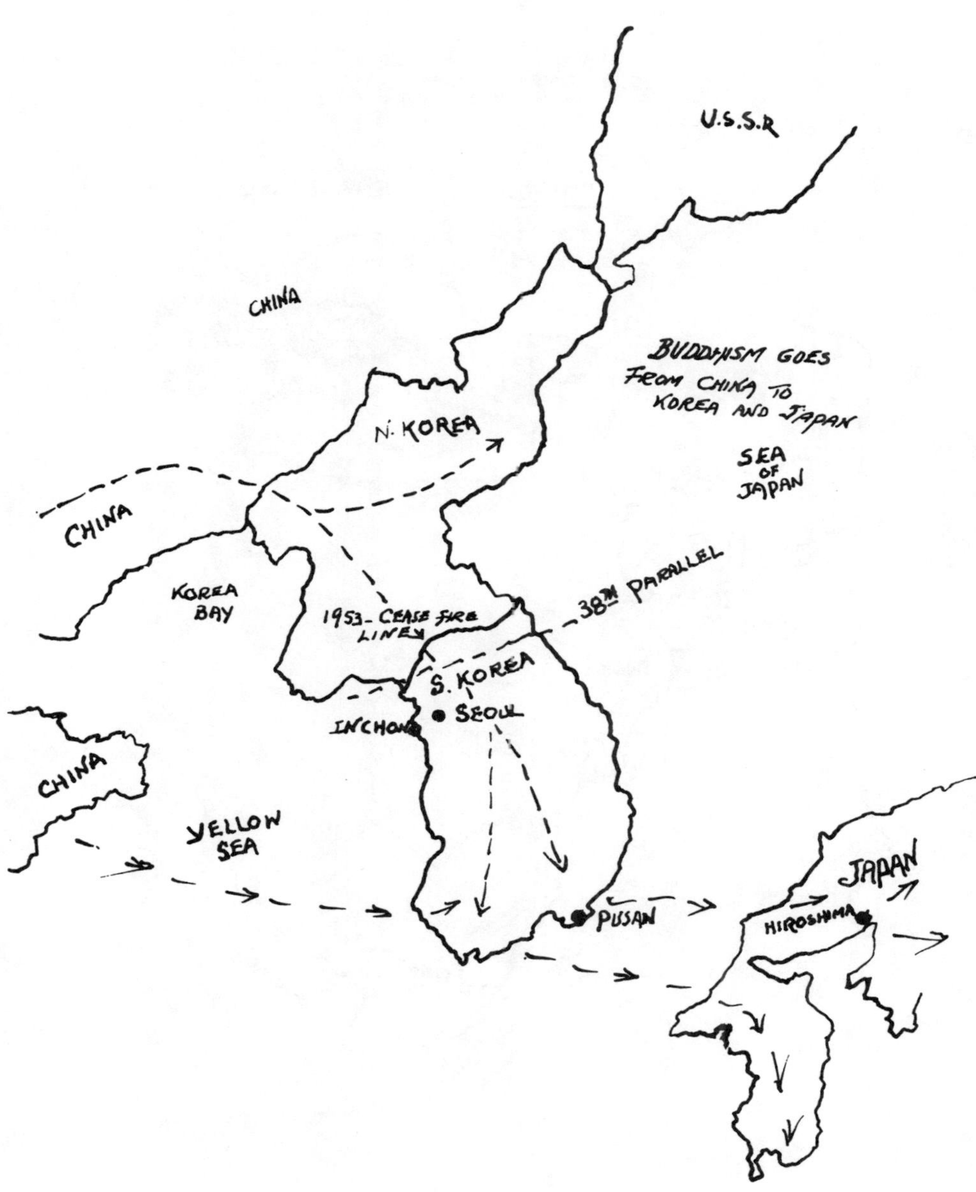
U.S.S.R
CHINA
BUDDHISM GOES
FROM CHINA TO
KOREA AND JAPAN
N. KOREA
SEA
OF
JAPAN
CHINA
KOREA
BAY
1953- CEASE FIRE
LINE
38TH PARALLEL
S. KOREA
INCHON
SEOUL
CHINA
YELLOW
SEA
PUSAN
JAPAN
HIROSHIMA

CONFUCIUS   551-479 B.C.
TODAY'S
CHINA
TIBET
NEPAL
BHUTAN
INDIA
BURMA
S.E. ASIA
CEYLON
GREAT WALL
PEKING
CHU FU
SHANGHAI
KOREA
JAPAN
PHILIPPINES
SINGAPORE
INDONESIA
BORNEO

Chapter XIV

Confucianism

As we continue our study of the principal religions of the Far East, we should get clearly in mind the time and place relationship of Siddartha Gautama, Confucius, and Lao-tze. The abbreviated summaries of the stories of these three "thinkers" as found in reference books are usually anchored to a common date—500 B.C. The casual reader gets the impression that they were good friends who met from time to time to share their views about the condition of man. To put our thoughts in order, let us look at their time and place relationship:

```
        650 B.C.    600 B.C.    550 B.C.    500 B.C.    450 B.C.
Buddha—India                      563                  483
Confucius—China                         551                  479
Lao-tze—China          604                     ?????
Chou Dynasty—770–256 B.C.
```

Buddha, a rebel against Hinduism, never left India. It was his philosophy about life that was carried throughout the Far East by his disciples, long after Buddha's death. His self-salvation belief became a religion, with Buddha the object of worship. It is obvious that he could not have met either of the two other sages. Under the limitations of communication in 500 B.C., it is doubtful that he had heard of Confucius and Lao-tze.

Confucius (Kung Fu-tsu) was an historical reality. His sixty years of wisdom were developed within a geographical area approximately like that shown by the rectangle on the accompanying map.

That superimposed rectangle on the map is a generous estimate of the area that was known with some intimacy to Confucius. Studies in world population growth suggest that the entire empire of China listed not more than 13,000,000 people in 500 B.C. The city of Beijing (Peking) today counts more than 10,000,000 citizens.

The first comment usually made about Confucianism is that it is NOT a religion. If we consider what Confucius gave his followers, it was indeed but a philosophy—a plan for maintaining an orderly society. It was a code of ethics. If, however, we consider what the passing years have made OUT of his teachings, we must acknowledge another world religion

Confucius (Kung Fu-tsu), born in 551 B.C., was the child of an aging military leader and a much younger mother. Upon his father's death when Confucius was but three years old, the responsibility for rearing the lad fell upon his mother. She was a most conscientious woman and had much personal influence upon her son's development. She died when he had turned twenty-two years of age. By that time, he had married a girl of his mother's selection, had completed such formal education as could be provided by tutors, and was ready to begin a career of public service.

Once in the public's eye, Confucius was seldom out of mind or sight of the people he was trying to help. His responsibilities ranged from "Supervisor of the Granaries"—a sort of "Joseph-in-Egypt" job—to positions of judicial authority. He was liked by some of his bosses and was exiled for periods of time by others. His chief difficulty lay not in poor performance but in his insistence upon standards so high that they became embarrassing and annoying to others.

He taught his disciple several areas of action and belief: 1. He taught that all persons are pure and good at birth; that man becomes evil only by the impurity of his environment; 2. Through obedience to Moral Laws man retains his own goodness; and 3. Faithfulness in observing the Moral Laws is the fundamental basis for good social order.

As he went about, teaching, he spoke constantly of justice, truth, charity, kindness, filial piety, and proper relations within the family. He said, "When universal virtue is practiced, the world is happy for all. Wise and capable men are elected to administrative office; sincerity and friendship are maintained.

"Thus man is kind, not only for his own children—the aged are cared for, the laborer is provided with congenial work; widows, orphans, and the infirm are well supported. Men and women live in tranquility.

Natural resources will not be wasted but developed for the furtherance of the public interest. Hence, all selfish devices will cease; robberies, thefts, and all other illegalities will disapear. The doors may safely be open day and night."

Clearly, this is not a religion. But a religion it became. This 2500-year-old message is one that we of the late twentieth century need to take to heart! As in the case of the Buddha, Confucius's followers so venerated the master teacher that he gained a degree of worship approaching that of a god. Temples in his honor dot the landscape of China today. Virtually every large city had its Confucian temple. Just what Confucius actually said or wrote is not known for certain, but his teachings were so thoroughly and voluminously set down by his students that we can have confidence in their accuracy.

Confucianism has at times been the official state religion of China. Annual ceremonies called for the veneration of this Chinese philosopher. In a period of corrupt governments, however, Confucianism was put down. The most recent example of such dereliction was that of Mao Tze-tung of today's People's Republic of China. He would have none of such society control. His "Red Guard" youth numbering millions got out of hand in their efforts to destroy the "good gifts" from past benefactors. Now, with recent changes in Chinese leadership, Confucius has been reinstated in the reviving intellectualism of the present. Confucian temples are now being restored as a part of China's cultural heritage.

It is inconceivable that the personality of the Great Sage should fade from memory and celebration as long as China endures. The Confucian temples are not crowded with altars overlooked by many gods. Only memorial tablets erected in his name or to the glory of his faithful students greet the temple visitor. A walk through the temple grounds in Peking becomes an inspiration. Even more impressive is the Confucian temple in Chu-fu, with its magnificently carved supporting columns of gray granite.

The tomb of Confucius is a huge mound of earth, unadorned. Before it stands the memorial tablet upon a platform of carved stone. Surrounding the temple at Chu-fu is a pine forest reserved as the burial site for the generations of the Kung family. Hundreds of simple earthen mounds rise from the ground beneath the trees.

The Kung family traces the descent of its members in direct line for seventy-six generations. Should you be privileged to visit the site, the chances are good that you will be appointed a guide who will show you the place that has been assigned to him at departure time.

When you have a few moments of free time, go to your school's librarian and ask that a copy of Confucius' *Analects* be placed upon the·reference shelf. You will not find it to be dull reading. We cannot but respect and honor the stern, personal righteousness of a man like Confucius.

The Upward Look

For years I've seen this temple's golden roof
And heard its bronze bells loudly ring, and yet
The mourning dove which perches on that branch
Knows more about this temple than do I.
Where I stretch lazily upon the ground,
I've come to know the temple from below.
The dove, intent on mating or on food,
Glides round and round these sacred grounds,
To perch an instant on that dragon's head,
To peek into its flaming eyes and mouth,
To soar straight through that belfry's open doors!
These things are easy for a dove to do.
Once I was seized with an insane desire
To climb out on those curving eaves
And gaze upon the mossy temple courts below,
But I was doomed to worship from the ground.
For years I've roamed these crumbling courts,
Have seen the roofs gleam in the midday sun,
And seen the pearly light of evening moon
Cast shadows in the darkening grove below.
Perhaps 'tis well that man look always up
To wonder what's beyond the lifted arch.
The unrevealed inspires eternal quest
And sends man's spirit on its Godward
Search for Truth.

Chapter XV

Taoism

The first statement to be made about Taoism is that it numbers among adherents about 20,000,000 people.

The second statement is that many scholars in the field of religious history doubt that the philosopher, Lao-tze, ever lived as an identifiable individual.

The third point to make is that some one initially began the writing of what is titled the *Tao Teh Ching*. How much of its contents are 2500 years old is not known. It has been discovered, however, that numerous philosophers between A.D. 400 and the close of the Manchu Dynasty in 1910 added their own beliefs and concerns over hundreds of years. That it may now properly be listed as one of the world's religions is certain. About 20,000,000 followers, mostly in China, enter its temples.

The *Tao Teh Ching* is a treasure house of meditative thinking, much of it, as elevated in thought and beautiful as can be found in the Bible of Judeo-Christianity. If one takes the time to read from it, he finds much evidence of belief in a Supreme Being. In other sections, however, the reader finds nothing beyond the mystical meditation of another Buddha who is seeking his own salvation through the desertion of life's inviting but deadly attractions. Many contemporary scholars, other than Chinese, have earned laurels and advanced degrees by making translations into English, French, German, and other modern languages of the Tao Teh Ching.

Surely the *Tao Teh Ching* was no haven of comfort to the masses of people 2500 years ago! They were almost totally illiterate. They worked as agrarians laying out their terraced fields, walking behind water buffalos in the muddy rice paddies, thatching the roofs of their mud houses, processing coconuts, and marketing the freshly netted fish. Those who lived farther north were harvesting their gaoliang, nuts, beets, radishes, cabbages, and turnips. They were storing the abundance of persimmons against the frigidity of winter and the blinding dust storms that swept down from the highlands of Mongolia.

No, not for the peasants! The very act of labor itself was probably their best protection from the depression and rejoicing of those who lived in the palaces. What they most needed was the availability of someone to whom they could appeal in times of distress. They wanted a god or, better still, many gods. As the Taoist temples began to dot the countryside, priests became the mediators between the gods and the people. The farmers, the fishermen, the cloth-makers, the brass finishers, and the bakers of breadstuff poured into the sanctuaries, lighted their sandalwood josh sticks before the altars, and touched their foreheads to the hard earth. Another world religion had been born. There were gods for the kitchen, for the marriage rites, for success in gambling, for the abundant harvest, for prosperity, good health and long life. Whatever the human need, help was at hand from a superior being. So far has the religion wandered from the original thinking of the mystics, that it is sometimes associated with Chinese folk religions.

By translation, "TAO" has the meaning of a road or highway. To the committed philosopher, life is indeed a highway. Having thought through the negative and positive facets of life, the Taoist sets forth boldly, his mind at peace, and no longer concerned about that great imponderable—the end of his physical life on earth.

***

If you, dear students, have been able to siphon from this profusion of words some small comprehension of the Taoist's pursuit of meaning in the universe, you have joined the company of scholars with advanced degrees! Your time for such meditation is limited by class assignments, sports, and club activities. Again, let us note that what you have struggled through has been for one purpose—to let you know that man, from the beginning of time and through all civilizations, has been a creature on quest for that which is greater than himself.

Now if you would like to know how long ago all these things took place, study this chart of the Dynasties of China.

Dynasties

ca. 2100–ca. 1600 B.C.	Xia (Hsia)	About 500 B.C.: "The
ca. 1600–1122 B.C.	Shang, or Yin	Buddha"—India
1122–770 B.C.	Western Zhou (Chou)	Lao-tze—China
770–256 B.C.	Eastern Zhou (Chou)	Kung Fu-tzu—China
	Spring and Autumn Period	(Confucius)
	770–476 B.C.	
	Warring States Period 475–221 B.C.	
	Han, Zhao (Chao), Wei, Yan (Yen), Qi	
	(Ch'i), Chu, Qin (Ch'in)	
221–207 B.C.	Qin (Ch'in)	
206 B.C.—A.D. 24	Western Han	
25–220	Eastern Han	
220–280	Period of the Three Kingdoms	
	Wei (North)	220–265
	Shu (Sichuan)	221–263
	Wu (South)	222–280
265–316	Western Jin (Chin)	
317–420	Eastern Jin (Chin)	
386–589	Period of the Southern and Northern	
	Dynasties	
	Southern Song (Sung)	420–479
	Southern Qi (Ch'i)	479–502
	Southern Liang	502–557
	Southern Chen	557–589
	Northern Wei	386–534
	Eastern Wei	534–550
	Northern Qi (Ch'i)	550–577
	Western Wei	535–556
	Northern Zhou (Chou)	557–581
581–618	Sui	
618–907	Tang	
907–979	Period of the Five Dynasties and Ten	
	Kingdoms	
	Later Liang	907–923
	Later Tang	923–936
	Later Jin (Chin)	936–946
	Later Han	947–950
	Later Zhou (Chou)	951–960
	Ten Kingdoms	907–979
960–1127	Northern Song (Sung)	
1127–1279	Southern Song (Sung)	
916–1125	Liao	

1115–1234	Jin (Chin)
1271–1368	Yuan, or Mongolian
1368–1644	Ming
1644–1911	Qing, or Manchu (Ch'ing) Death of the last Qing emperor, 1967
1912–1949	Republic of China
1949	People's Republic of China

Lao-tze remains a figure more legendary than provably dated. Rumors that circulated long ago of an actual meeting with Confucius are unreliable, although by the lifelines above, such a meeting could have taken place. What cannot be disputed is that these three "thinkers" were the progenitors of beliefs and practices which subsequently were embraced by hundreds of millions of human beings.

And now, to Confucius. We can be certain that the land mass of Confucius's China was not much different from what it is today. "Continental Drift," of which you have surely been informed in your classes in geography, was already very ancient natural history. What you must try to fix in mind is that this oft-quoted (Confucius say!) instructor in human relationships was walking about in that rectangle on the preceding map more than 2500 years ago! Great Jehoshophat! That was a long time ago, wasn't it? (Excuse me! You are probably wondering what Jehoshophat has to do with the China scene. Let me explain. When I was about your present age, we had assembled quite a few terms that served to emphasize our moments of strong feeling. Since we had been brought up to respect instruction from our elders, we were familiar with "Thou shalt not take the name of the Lord in vain."We soon created our own expletives. "Holy Moses!" was another effective outburst. These may not have been in good taste, but they did not violate our "bringing up.")

Come to think of it, Jehoshophat was not a bad choice for this page. He had been the King of Judah—849–837 B.C. He was already serving the Jewish Jehovah before Confucius appeared. He had ruled over Jerusalem for twenty-five years—"doing what was right in the sight of the Lord." I must admit that you young people of today have an advantage which we hesitated to use—you know—First Amendment rights? Just this past week I was watching an R film on television, prime time. The actors and actresses had a marvelous time tossing God, his son, Jesus, and Hell all over the stage set! One can't help wondering if the change indicates significant progress in human communication. What do you think?

Confucius was born and died in Chu Fu in Shantung Province.

Since Buddha never got to China personally, he could not possibly have met Confucius and Lao-tze. It is well to note that the three thinkers never escaped from their humanist faith in man. Their followers made gods out of each, with temples, priests, and nuns.

Although a small segment of the Great Wall may date from 215 B.C., most of its 1500-mile length was built after A.D. 1368. Confucius and Lao Tze never had a chance to walk on the wall. Within the past five years, the tourists, with cameras dangling, far outnumber the half-million ancient laborers who so carefully created this "Wonder of the World."

As a reward for your patience, here are some interesting parallels:

Tao Teh Ching	**Bible**
Be humble and you will remain entire. Be bent, and you will remain straight. . . . Be worn, and you will remain new. . . . He who has little will receive. He who has much will be embarrassed.	Blessed are the meek, for they shall inherit the earth. Blessed are the poor in spirit for theirs is the kingdom of heaven. But I say unto you, love your enemies. . . . do good to them that hate you. For my yoke is easy and my burden is light.
Return love for great hatred.	And now abideth faith, hope, and love. . . . but the greatest of these is love.
My words are very easy to know and very easy to practice. . . . He who defends with love will be secure. Heaven will save him and protect him.	

Chapter XVI

Shintoism

A brief review, please, in the manner of the soap operas and "Masterpiece Theater"—just in case you skipped some earlier pages.

When the Indian Buddhist monks, converts from Hinduism, crossed the Himalayas into China in A.D. 65, they could not have imagined either the acceptance of their beliefs or the geographical expansion that would follow their missionary efforts. That was nearly 2000 years ago. Lao-tze and Confucius had been dead for more than 300 years.

You may find these figures boring, but I emphasize their importance because readers of history have trouble developing a sensitivity to the slow passage of time. For instance, consider again the chart of the Chinese dynasties a few pages back. Four thousand years were covered in one page! You can't take in something like that in three minutes. That chart represents about 300 generations of human beings!

To you seniors, World War II, Korea, and Vietnam are events covered in your classroom work. You may have had some further word about them from your fathers, uncles, or grandfathers. To you, the assassination of Abraham Lincoln is ancient history—120 years ago. The important point to be made here is that, despite the rise and fall of dynasties, monarchies, and primitive tribalism, man's compulsion to worship survives.

On a recent trip to the Far East, when taking shelter from a sudden shower, I stepped onto an area of terrazzo flooring. Overhead, the thatched roof leaked. In fascination, I watched the initial puddle of water broaden. The pool expanded slowly in all directions, but particularly toward the outer edge of the floor where it dropped to a lower

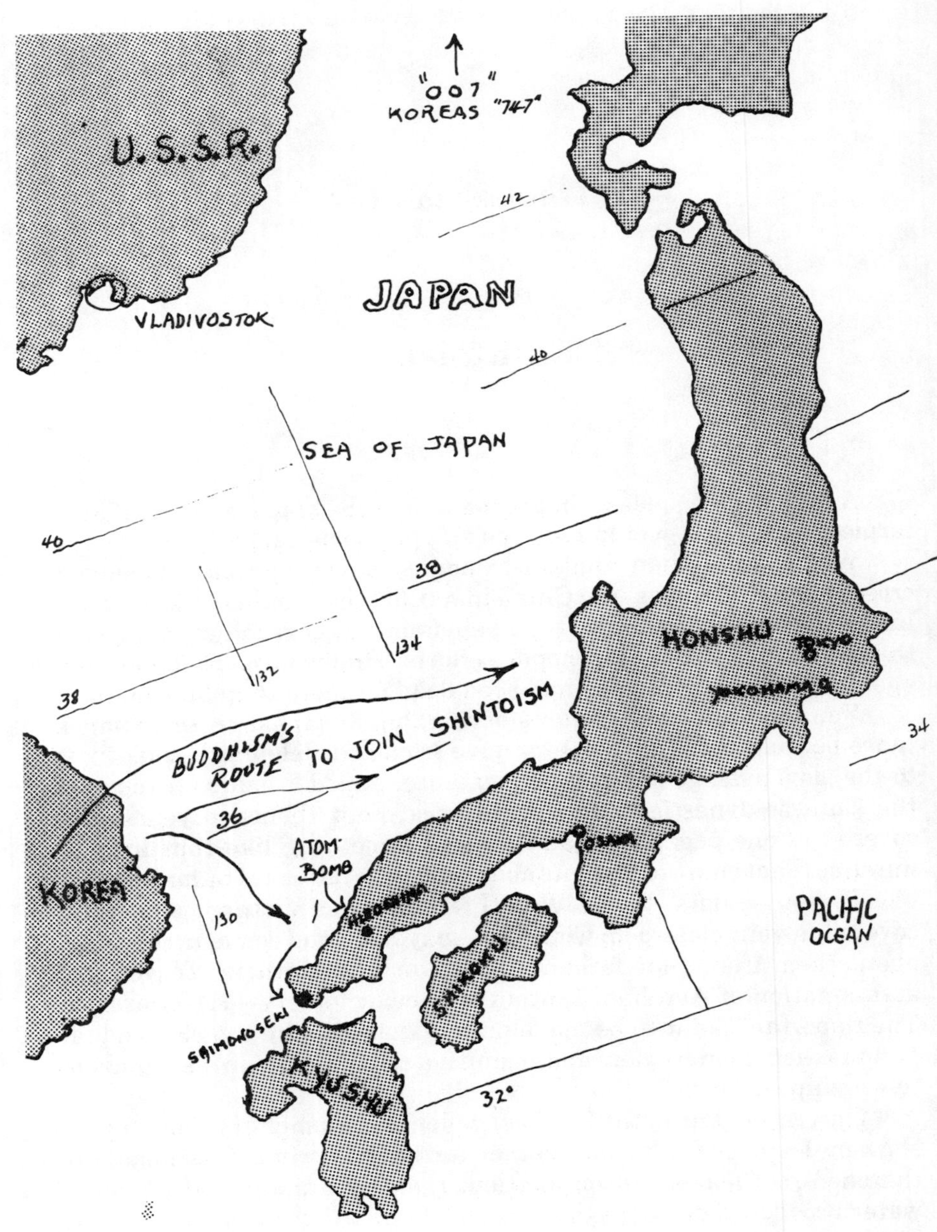
U.S.S.R.
VLADIVOSTOK
"007"
KOREAS "747"
JAPAN
42
40
SEA OF JAPAN
40
38
134
132
38
HONSHU
TOKYO
YOKOHAMA
34
BUDDHISM'S ROUTE TO JOIN SHINTOISM
36
ATOM BOMB
OSAKA
KOREA
130
HIROSHIMA
SHIKOKU
PACIFIC OCEAN
SHIMONOSEKI
KYUSHU
32°

level and continued in an increasing stream to the curbside.

In my mind's eye, the wet terrazzo floor became the land mass of China and Southeast Asia. The fragments of broken straw that had fallen from the thatch above became the Buddhist monks who drifted slowly outward—some to the north and others to Malaysia and the islands beyond. The shower ended as suddenly as it had come. Those who were with me gingerly sidestepped the Buddhist stream and went their ways. How little did they know what they had missed!

Well, that's about the way Buddhism spread throughout Asia, running through accessible valleys and over ranges of mountains to set up a working arrangement with Confucianism and Taoism. Together they provided an assortment of temples and a variety of gods in later years that would have startled the founders. People could worship almost anywhere with ease. There were periods of persecution, but also times of joy, depending upon the whims of the emperors and princes who held power. Occasionally, one or another of the religions would be elevated to the position of state religion, only to fall back into relative obscurity.

When Buddhism moved into Korea, a land famous for its craggy mountains and rushing torrents, the people were largely worshipers of nature. Spirits occupied the trees, the rocks, and the rivers. Some revered their ancestors as did the Confucians. The term for nature-worship is "shamanism," a derivative of the Chinese language indicating the peasant's appeal to one of priestly capacity for communication with the spirits.

Since we have already made brief reference to Korea, we shall add but a little more to fill out the picture before moving on to Shintoism. Your study of contemporary American history has covered the Korean conflict of 1949–53. Communism, an extension of the Moscow theme, had swept down into Korea with the full support of "volunteers" from Mao Tze-tung's recently acquired China. While the struggle of resistance was nominally under the heading of "United Nations," our country provided both the manpower and the money for the resistance.

For nearly one hundred years before the Communist takeover, the Christian missions of the free world had been active in Korea. The work was intensified following the defeat of the Japanese in World War II. Medical schools, hospitals, and schools for general education were spread over the country. In no other country in the world have Christian missions been so welcomed. Below is another chart which enlarges the information provided by the earlier one.

153

	North Korea		South Korea	
Non-religious	9,335,000	52%	187,000	.05%
Shamanists	2,796,000	15.6%	9,715,400	25.9%
Buddhists	300,000	1.7%	5,804,000	15.5%
Confucianists	none		4,980,000	13.3%
Atheists	2,832,300	15.8%	9,000	.0002%
Christians	161,900	.09%	11,409,800	30.5%
Population	17,926,000		37,444,000	

In North Korea, 12,168,000 are "disinterested" in religion.

In South Korea, 196,000 are "disinterested" in religion.

NOTE: Religious people often "go underground" when communism moves in.

Shintoism

We now turn to Shintoism and to its union (in a sense) with Buddhism, the invader.

As to ethnic origin of the Japanese, we know far less than about the Chinese. The Japanese themselves left no written records prior to the eighth century A.D. Upon the arrival of Buddhism with its scholarly monks came also a remarkable tool—the Chinese character language. The Chinese had been using it for more than 2000 years.

Quickly putting this new skill to use, the Japanese created two accounts of their own civilization: The Kojiki—A.D.712 and The Nihongi—A.D. 720.

From these we learn the origin of Shintoism. The Japanese word can be separated into "Shin" and "To." These two syllables are identical with "Shen Tao"—the "Way of the Gods" in Chinese. The "Tao" is the same "Tao," or road, that Lao-tze talked about.

In the origins of most religions, one finds, as we have noted before, that the "supernaural" quickly takes over, even though it was lacking at the time of founding. The story in Japan is not different. Taking what gods the traveling monks had brought with them, the Japanese brought in their own "Amaterasu," the Sun Goddess. It was she who, in her omiscience, created the island kingdom below by dropping pearls of creativity into the blue waters of the Pacific. It is natural to expect that Amaterasu would take over the commanding position in the religious heirarchy. Thus the first emperor of Japan was considered a grandson of the Sun Goddess, initiating a succession of such rulers by divine appointment. Until the end of World War II, the divine images of the royal couple were so revered that faces were turned away from the emperor and empress whenever they made sortie from the palace grounds—whether in Kyoto or in Tokyo. They dared not look upon the brilliance of the divine rulers.

Being descended from the Sun Goddess, the female offspring of the royal couple were accorded status equal to that of males. For centuries, women of Japan were honored to a degree not seen in many other world religions. Japan's defeat in 1945 did much to shake this divine loyalty; but not even the American occupation and the democratization of Japan have been able to eliminate the long-cultivated loyalty to the royal family.

The companionship that developed between Shinto and Buddhism cannot be adequately emphasized in these lines. The two religions adjusted to each other and have lived in relative peace—side by side—for centuries. How different from the antagonism in India between the Moslems and the Hindus! Let this be an invitation to the curious to learn more fully about one of the most significant socioreligious happenings in history.

With the passage of time, Shintoism became increasingly the embodiment of national patriotism. This produced an almost fanatic belief in the divine destiny of the Japanese people and had much to do with the attack on our country in 1941. With all that has happened since then, you are familiar. Japan has become a giant industrial plant, now challenging us economically and even culturally.

To visit the Japanese in their own country has been one of my life's privileges. Since 1922, there have been twenty-two such meetings, both before and after the modification of the divine image of the emperor. Their inherited characteristics, whether from Mongoloid strains out of northeast Asia or from ancestors who once lived in the tropical islands of the South Pacific, reveal the Japanese to be of high intelligence and creativity and possessing an inborn determination not to be ignored as the world of nations becomes ever more intimate.

A final observation at this point: As an American schoolboy, reared in the wonderful days of the public schools of five different states, I came early to learn something about the Greeks, the Romans, the Egyptians, and the barbaric background of Europe. I also knew something of the developments of religious conflict in the Near and Middle East, since I was raised in the Judeo-Christian traditions. Ancient history had always been a favorite subject.

Little had I learned, however, of the Far East. It remained a clouded area, exotic and unknowable to an American schoolboy. A lifetime of observation has changed that. I suggest now that the unfolding years will find America looking increasingly across the waters of the Pacific. Despite our present involvemens in the Mediterranean area and in Central America, we shall be dealing with about two billion, five hundred million human beings along a line extending from Japan, through the Far East, and on to Australia and New Zealand.

Good history teachers will be in great demand!

Chapter XVII

Echoes from Earlier Chapters

Yes, Shinto is the last of eleven religions that were nominated for study as we opened this book for the first time. In those early pages, a statistical position was taken that the United States of America was, at the time of its founding, a nation of men, women, and children spiritually nourished by a belief in God as Creator of all that is, and also in His son, Jesus Christ; that the son walked among men in human form until recalled by God, the Father, who dwelt in Heaven, a place the beauty of which was beyond man's descriptive powers.

We examined the evidence from the founding documents of a new nation that, with God's help, would found a new political society dedicated to equality among all citizens and to their freedom to hold and to express their religious beliefs without government's interference. Especially did their Constitution make clear that no religious organization should ever, as Church of State, dictate or influence the making of laws by which the enfranchised citizens were to be governed. Such laws would thus spring from the quality of the moral codes held by the voting citizens as reflected in the judgments of their elected representatives in the Congress of the United States and in all lower orders of government.

It is statistically demonstrated that the young nation was one which, although overwhelmingly populated by people of Christian commitment, welcomed other religious adherents to citizenship without prejudicial restraints. It bore testimony to the revolutionary concept that all men are the children of God, the Father of mankind, and brothers one to another. America was indeed a Christian nation, without the encumbrance of a Church of State.

Conceivably, the citizen ratio between Christian and other religous adherents could shift. Despite the arrival of more than 50,000,000 immigrants during our 210 years of freedom, and the birthright citizenship of their children and grandchildren, more than 90 percent of the young people sitting in the classrooms of our tax-suported public schools represent families of Christian affiliation. It can still be truthfully said that the United States of America is a Christian nation devoid of discriminatory intent.

How well or how poorly we have performed under that commitment is indeed subject to challenge. In world history, there has never been a nation—or body of people less formally titled—that has attained its stated ideals. Power and material prosperity dilute the original moral imperatives. At first, under the excitement of and enthusiasm for the ennobling quest, literature, the fine arts, and scientific research soar to unexpected heights. Then come the material rewards, the "good life," and the first faltering steps of indifference to an earlier allegiance. Literature, the fine arts, and science become imitative rather than creative. The glory that was Babylon, Egypt, Greece, Rome, and the Tang Dynasty fades. The life-style prevails, even to its own subsequent destruction. The ennobling quest moves on to other peoples—testing, testing, testing.

This is recorded history, not fancy. The Founding Fathers were not illiterate. When they stepped ashore in America 400 years ago, they were on quest. When they assembled in Independence Hall, Philadelphia, they announced in ringing words the reliance of the new nation upon the Providence of God. Through the passing years, the nation has faltered, stumbled, regained its balance and held fast to its faith in a Supreme Being who oversees the affairs of men.

Do we believe in this America? In our abundance, prosperity, and leadership of the free world, are we abandoning the moral codes inherent in our religious traditions? Shall the historian a thousand years from now rewrite that line to read "The glory that once was Babylon, Egypt, Greece, Rome, Tang, and the United States?"

World Population ...4,373,917,535
Christianity 1,432,686,519
Islam 722,956,504
Nonreligious 715,901,416
Hinduism 582,949,920
Buddhism 273,715,590
Ch. Folk Rel. 197,795,366
Atheism 195,119,360
New Religions 96,021,800
(Cults, et cetera)

158

Tribal Rel. 89,963,450
Taoism 20,000,000
Judaism 16,938,230
Sikhism 14,244,360
Shamanism 13,502,77
Confucianism 4,980,000
Bahaimis 3,822,630
Shintoism 3,526,380
Jainism 3,243,000
Afro. Amer. Spir. 3,100,000
Spiritists 2,374,440
Parsis 154,220

With the preceding statistics handy, we now narrow the focus of our picture and concentrate on the three religions which have areas of both agreement and disagreement:Christianity, Judaism, and Islam. These are facts, not theories:

1. Both Christianity and Mohammedanism are theologically rooted in Judaism.
2. The three religions are monotheistic. They attribute omniscience to God as Creator of the universe and of all living creatures on this earth. He is the Ultimate Judge of the quality of a person's life on earth when a Day of Judgment shall arrive.
3. The three religions assert the reality of *heaven* and *hell* as associated with reward or punishment.Their descriptions of these places vary greatly.
4. Sin, they agree, is that which violates God's rules for living a commendable life within the total community of human beings.
5. They reject the belief of Secular Humanism that the human being represents the highest stage in evolutionary progress—that man, if inclined to worship, should honor himself.
6. The adherents of the three faiths have all been subjected to persecution and restriction at the hands of Communism.

While noting the commonalities of the three religions, we should also consider their differences. Friction and conflict do not spring from areas of agreement. They seem to thrive on opposing points of view and practice.

1. Christianity asserts the brotherhood of all human beings, nourished in an atmosphere of love, without political restraints or religious favoritism. It propagates by example and persuasion—not by compulsion. Its periodic failures to measure up to this high idealism

have been well recorded in history, but the quality and direction of its commitment remain the continuing objective of its fallible performance. It supports repentance and forgiveness.

2. Mohammedanism, whenever conditions are favorable, insists on being both religion and the state. The Koran is its rule book for both personal and governmental guidance. Courts of law in our democratic sense do not exist. When in a position of governmental authority, it places other religions, when not specifically excluded, under limiting restrictions. Its opposition to the Jewish people and to their political existence as a nation is historical.

3. Judaism, both as faith and political reality, presents the religious historian with a dilemma. As you have already learned, the Jewish people, of a common faith, are resident—often with citizenship status, in more than one hundred countries that are members of the United Nations. They are at least united by their faith if not politically and geographically.

Now, however, there is a world Jewish political center. It is the nation of Israel. Since the break-up of the Kingdom of David 2000 years ago, Judaism's followers have wandered over the face of the earth, making their remarkable contributions to literature, science, and industry.

Suddenly, as historical time moves, the close of World War II brought about the negotiated establishment (1948) of the new nation—Israel. It is the one country in the world where Jewish religion and government are in control of the people's destiny. In a limited sense, therefore, the "diaspora" was ended. The Jewish people have come home once again.

Let us examine the religious statistics of the new nation of Israel (1980).

```
JEWS ...................................................................................................3,401,000
Moslems ................................................................................................307,400
Christians .................................................................................................85,100
Nonreligious ............................................................................................50,000
Atheists ......................................................................................................1,600
Bahai'is ........................................................................................................600
Others .........................................................................................................1,300
                                                                                               3,847,000
```

The return of Jews to their regained homeland was initially in considerable volume, often under great difficulties. They fled from sites of Jewish persecution in Europe; they came from Arab countries. (Conversely, many Moslems left Israel. In many aspects, the scene paralleled what took place when the division of India created Pakistan as a religious haven for Mohammedanism.)

Despite the provision of the new government that any Jew would be granted Israeli citizenship upon return, immigration from other countries where Jews were living satisfactorily was more limited. This is what the current situation offers:

World Judaism	17,000,000
Israel	3,401,000
Elsewhere	13,599,000

What makes the situation unique is that the historic exclusivity of Judaism has been that of a nation that is both religiously and governmentally embracive of all human beings who were born into Judaism. They are not a missionary religion. They wanted to be together as a nation as in days of yore. Their expansion in numbers has always been by biological reproduction—not by conversion. In this respect Judaism matches the Hindus and the Jains.

By contrast, Christianity has never had the concept of a world center for Christianity, governmentally authoritative. Christianity is a spiritual unity of believers wherever they may happen to reside in nations of disparate political types.

This is not the place to discuss the international and religious confusion that today wrenches Israel, that tiny geographical segment of the Near East. What is taking place bears eloquent testimony to the necessity of combining religious and political history in the classrooms of our American schools.

A final comment about Mohammedanism—it DOES have a world religious center for Islam—Mecca in Saudi Arabia. A pilgrimage to the Kaaba at least once in a lifetime is urged upon all adherents. Failing that personal achievement, the worshiper may delegate the pilgrimage to another agent. Obviously there is neither need nor want for Moslems to "come home." Every Moslem state is "home"—a center for both worship and governmental operational control.

All other religionists are interested in finding the answer to one specific question: How tolerant are the several Islamic states to the influx of non-Moslems who wish to spread their faiths, to build colleges and seminaries, open medical schools and hospitals, and worship without fear of governmental interference? Here, once more, we turn to statistics for enlightenment. In those nations that we loosely refer to as Christian nations—where Christianity is the dominant religion—we find a Christian total of 1,337,235,000—(85 percent) living in brotherhood with 223,360,000—(15 percent) Moslems.

The total is 1,560,595,000 of the combined brotherhood.

Now let us reverse the statistics. In what we loosely call Islamic countries—those in which Mohammedanism is the dominant faith:

503,015,000 ....93.7% Moslems
 33,810,000 .... 6.3% Christians

536,835,000 ....The Combined Brotherhood.

The figures become even more informative when we note that the Christian populations in countries now predominantly Islamic expanded when those same countries were under the influence or political control of European nations in the nineteenth and twentieth centuries:

		Formerly under:
Algeria	152,470	(France)
Bangladesh	449,960	(England)
Chad	1,476,000	(France)
Egypt	7,543,840	(England)
Indonesia	17,069,000	(Netherlands)
		(England)
		(France)
		(HInduism)
		(Buddhism)
Jordan	112,760	(England)
Malaysia	861,000	(England)
Mali	120,000	(France)
Mauritania	6,060	(France)
Morocco	102,300	(France)
		(Spain)
Niger	19,120	(France)
Pakistan	1,475,000	(England)
Qatar	16,000	(England)
Senegal	285,630	(France)
Somalia	2,270	(England)
		(Italy)
Sudan	1,939,300	(Anglo-Egypt.)
Tunisia	22,760	(France)
Total Christians	31,653,470	

Under the earlier influence or occupation by European nations, Christian missionary activity was given a free hand. Thus, the current domination by Mohammedanism over Christians came as an "inheritance factor." They have had to live with Christians whether or not they would have chosen to do so. If we now subtract this "inheritance" from the present figures in predominantly Moslem populations, we discover:

Christians in Moslem countries 33,819,614
Christians by "inheritance" under England & France 31,653,470
Others 1,166,144

One may conclude rather quickly that there has not been much welcome extended to Christian missionary activity since the close of World War II. Such growth as is revealed has come from normal population increase—not from Christian missionary efforts.

To arrange statistics in this way is not intended to condone the European takeover of other countries nor to lessen the indictment of the western world's participation in the slave trade. What the figures do show conclusively is that history cannot be taught intelligently unless accompanied by the history of religions.

We may also conclude that our Moslem brothers, although joining with Christians and others in condemning communism's restrictions, are at the same time content to place their own restrictions upon all religions outside the covers of the Koran.

We turn now in the next chapter to the Communist world.

Chapter XVIII

Communism

It must be obvious to you students that a story about the religions of the world and their involvement with political history cannot be laid out in a neat chronological line. The progression is often "put on hold" while one briefly registers some events far removed in time, place, and cultures with which an important union will later be made. It is a zigzag course that constantly challenges the memory of the side trips.

You have had brief mention of communism earlier. Now we shall fill in some of the details. Today's communism is a twentieth-century version of ages-old efforts to persuade the people that a few select persons, if given the authority—or, if not given, then taken—can run the poliical show better than it could be run under a shared authority. Out of the Marx-Lenin partnership, which resulted in the overthrow of the old Romanoff Constitutional Monarchy in 1917–1918, came the USSR of which you hear and read so much today. That revolution was relatively fast. Some confusion was exhibited in the initial takeover, and hundreds of lives were lost, including those of Czar Nicholas and his royal family. They were summarily executed as "enemies of the people."

Again I must make clear that this little book does not have as an objective the narration of the details of the Russian revolution nor of the subsequent international violence of World War II when Adolf Hitler attempted his own version of "rule by the selected few." Your own history teachers should have given you such information. What we need to do here is to set forth clearly the philosophy of the Communist movement and to report on its implementation and progress during the sixty-nine years of its operations. We shall bypass those endless negotiations between the Russians and their three allies—Britain, France, and the United States—after the defeat of Nazi Germany. First let us look at the dimensions of the USSR and the communist countries around the world in population, area, religionists, and the non-religious.

The population figures have been obtained by averaging an assortment of estimates in various publications—almanacs, atlases, encyclopedias. For our purposes, these figures are informative rather than exact. Land areas also vary from one source to another. Overall, however, the results are acceptable for a general picture of world realities.

COUNTRY	Land Area (Sq. m.)	Population	Religionists
Afghanistan	250,000	22,000,000	21,000,000
Albania	11,000	2,800,000	750,000
Angola	480,000	7,200,000	7,000,000
Benin	43,000	3,500,000	3,450,000
Bulgaria	42,000	8,800,000	6,800,000
Cambodia	70,000	9,500,000	9,000,000
China	3,700,000	1,004,000,000	300,000,000
Congo	130,000	1,600,000	1,500,000
Cuba	44,000	10,000,000	9,500,000
Czechoslovakia	50,000	15,000,000	12,000,000
Ethiopia	470,000	33,000,000	30,000,000
East Germany	42,000	16,800,000	15,000,000
Hungary	36,000	10,800,000	9,000,000
Laos	90,000	3,800,000	3,500,000
Mongolia	600,000	1,750,000	600,000
Mozambique	300,000	10,600,000	10,350,000
Nicaragua	80,000	2,400,000	2,200,000
North Korea	47,000	18,000,000	6,000,000
Poland	121,000	35,800,000	32,000,000
Romania	92,000	22,500,000	18,965,000
USSR	8,650,000	270,000,000	133,800,000
Vietnam	130,000	55,000,000	50,000,000
Yemen, South	110,000	2,000,000	1,970,000
Yugoslavia	98,000	22,600,000	18,550,000
	15,686,000	1,589,450,000	652,935,000

Again using rounded-off figures, we discover some very interesting facts about the expansion of Communism.

Land area of the earth estimated at (100%)   57,000,000 Square miles
Communist countries occupy (26.3%)   15,000,000 Square miles
World population estimated at   4,375,000,000
People under Communism (36%)   1,590,000,000

The term "religionists" includes all holding of beliefs and practices, from the most primitive to the most formal. The figures which follow are probably too generous with respect to the number of atheists, communists, and other unbelievers.

People under Communism   1,590,000,000
Religionists   652,935,000

The Communist party members and others   937,065,000

The worldwide membership in the Communist Party provides no reliable figures for its world membership. Those active in running the various governments are but a fraction of the 937,065,000 given above. The Communist states listed above hold, probably against their will, more than 650,000,000 human beings who practise their assorted faiths under varying degrees of persecution and restriction.

Study carefully the next map. Countries under Communist governments vary considerably as to the controls and restrictions under which religions must live. An interesting class project would be the assignment of certain countries, either in Eurasia or Africa, to the class members for study and report.

Religion Versus Anti-Religion in the World—1984

The darkened areas of this map represent Communist-governed people, either by one-party Communist states or by Socialist states which are atheistic. Statistically, the figures are:

Population-DARK AREAS 1,590,000,000
Atheists, Non. Religious 937,065,000
Religionists   652,935,000

The white areas on this map represent those countries which offer religious freedom, in some cases with minor restrictions related to local conditions.

The recent conflict between the government of India and the Sikhs illustrates how local problems may lead to religious restrictions in a

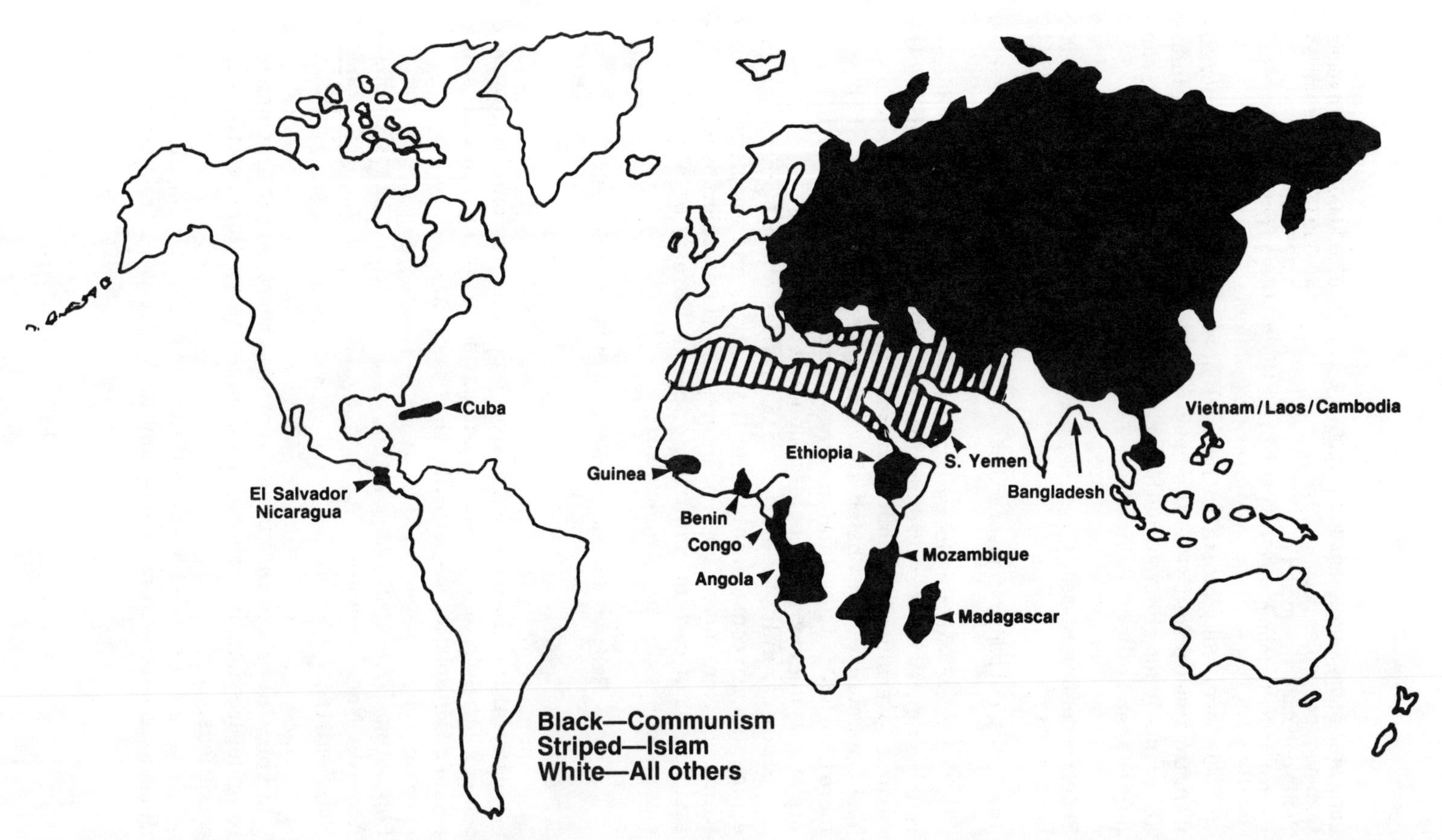

Vietnam / Laos / Cambodia
Bangladesh
S. Yemen
Ethiopia
Guinea
Benin
Congo
Angola
Mozambique
Madagascar
Cuba
El Salvador
Nicaragua
Black—Communism
Striped—Islam
White—All others

country which guarantees religious liberty. Certain South and Central American countries give similar evidence.

Those figures should help you to understand why our country is facing such tremendous immigration problems.

The areas marked with cross-lines represent roughly states which are governed by Moslems.

The irony of the current situation can be quickly grasped by considering the following statements:

1. The Communist one-party states, controlled by the selected few who manage public voting, are against ALL religions with intent to destroy.

2. ALL religions oppose Communism.

3. Mohammedanism places restrictions against ALL religions other than its own.

4. Christianity offers total security against government's interference with religious freedom and practice.

Do not confuse pure socialism with communism. The two terms are vastly different. Socialism in its broadest sense works to obtain an equitable distribution of the world's natural resources among all the people. To accomplish this purpose, it places various degrees of limitation upon what is called private ownership. This can be seen in government's ownership, or management, of banks, transportation, forests, lakes, minerals, postal services, and so on. It discourages, or forbids, private ownership of such resources. Whatever the degree of government management, many socialist countries do permit areas of "free enterprise."

Communism is absolute control by a selected few of virtually everything. A communist state is a one-party unit that dictates the lives of all citizens and maintains control by military power, voting procedures, and a court system totally at variance with democracy's administration of justice. In a way it is a parallel to an ABSOLUTE MONARCHY. It is as restrictive as were the Nazi and Fascist movements of Hitler and Mussolini. There have been examples of benevolent monarchies where the treatment of citizens has been sufficiently liberal as to discourage revolution. In countries of limited population, such governing has long been tolerated. (Contemporary examples are Bahrain, Jordan, Morocco, Nepal, Oman, Saudi Arabia, and Swaziland.)

What we have to keep in mind, however, is that there is no such thing as benevolent communism. It is as ruthless, cruel, amoral, and spontaneous as is necessary to maintain its authority. It has internationally proclaimed its atheistic intention to eliminate religion as an antique historical superstition that interferes with man's ability to govern himself. There is no God! Period! From the Baltic sea in western Europe to the Pacific Ocean, facing Japan and Alaska, Communism holds sway. From the Arctic expanse of Siberia to the very boundary of Iran it measures its land control. From its widespread political maneuvering and subversion it now controls five governments in Africa. Cuba fell to its operations in 1959. Grenada was about to join the list when American intervention restored democracy. Nicaragua has a Communist government, and El Salvador might follow the same route if America is unsuccessful in its Central American efforts.

As you read the news in the daily papers and weekly magazines, be alert for coverage of events taking place in governments that appear to be in transition from one type to another. The governments listed below are all members of the United Nations.

The reasons for these sudden changes, or reversals, are many:

1) The takeover group, without necessarily wishing to change the type of government—democratic, socialist, or dictatorship—believes that they can do the job better than those currently in power.
2) The takeover group fears the loss of the prevailing type of government by subversion from within.
3) The takeover group intends to secure the governing power by throwing out the incumbent leaders.
4) The incumbent government declares martial law in order to prevent the possibility of its overthrow.

These and other variations are occurring continually in today's world. The outcomes may be important to our own free society. You can understand why most of these little revolutions are taking place in Africa. Long accustomed to the colonial status under European control, the released subjects following World War II wanted to set up in their own countries governments that they believed would correct the inequities and injustices which they had experienced. Sudden seizure is the handiest weapon, for all insurgents find that they are faced with religious prejudices with which they must deal. The issues are quite clear: Shall we compromise between "East" and "West," or shall we go "all out" for communism or democratic government?

A very stimulating class project could result from the selection by each member of one of the countries appearing in this list. Go to your history teachers and librarians to discover the best reference sources; scan the daily newspapers for dated events. Read the summaries in the weekly newsmagazines. If your class enrollment includes students whose families have international backgrounds, invite a friend to examine with you the conditions prevailing in a given country. And keep in mind that you are privileged to live in a nation where such research is welcomed.

Nations in Transition

The dates following each name refer to the latest events leading to the current situation.

Algeria—1965   A one-party Socialist regime with predominantly Moslem religious background

Bangladesh—1975   The result of the partitioning of India; predominantly Moslem constituency

Bolivia—1981   Military rule

Brazil—1964   Military rule

Burundi—1966   Military junta; poverty stricken; overpopulated

Chad—1982   Military junta; conflict between Libya and France

Chile—1973   Military junta

El Salvador—1984   In transition from military to civilian rule

Equitorial Guinea—1979   Military coup; thousands killed

Ethiopia—1978   Long the empire under Haile Selassie; Moslem and Christian conflict; Russia and Cuba involved

Ghana—1972–1982   Several military coups

Guinea—1958   Militant one-party state

Honduras—1972   Republic under military control

Iraq   One-party Socialist/military state; Moslems predominate

Liberia—1980   Military coup; a nation founded by children of American slave-days

Libya—1969   Military dictatorship; Muammar Qaddafi, dictator

Mali—1974   Military dictatorship

Nicaragua—1984   Now a Marxist government

Niger—1974   Military junta

Panama—1968   A republic under military rule

Peru—1968   Socialist military rule

Philippines—1972   One-party republic under "Martial Law"

The countries listed above are a sampling of the governments in transition, particularly in the "third world" nations. Do have an interesting time in the library!

A Wish

I wish that I by seeking well might find
A portion of the grace God gives the flower,
That I by drinking might imbibe
The calm and quiet of the twilight hour,
That from each day's frenetic strife I might acquire
The stately tenor of the sunset's fire.

I wish that I in some way might inherit
A fraction of the beauty of the hills,
That daily I might gain a tiny share
Of the rippling, singing laughter of the rills,
That o'er my shameful soils and stains would flow
The purity and whiteness of the snow.

The mighty seas, the mountains, and the fields,
The trees, the sleeping valleys, and the sky—
These freely given gifts of Heaven I find
Much simpler, yet more beautiful than I.

Fond hope! That fellowmen in me may trace
The lovely, peaceful quiet of His face!

L.R.S.
1926

Chapter XIX

The Missionary Movement

One can be reasonably certain that most high school students have seen one or more television episodes of "Mission Impossible." If the student has been so underprivileged as never to have been offered Latin in his curriculum, then there is not much point in dwelling on the verb *mitto*—to send. In the broadest sense, a missionary is someone who "has been sent" on a mission. He has a message to deliver or some action to perform. It might be to carry food to starving people, or to deliver a confidential document to a government representative living abroad. It could even be the secret movement of an international spy to transmit information to another similar agent.

Most of you students come from religious backgrounds wherein you have learned about, and perhaps seen or heard, special representatives of your family's religion who have been sent to tell other people about your religion. These persons are popularly known to the English-speaking world as "missionaries." They have also gone forth from countries like Norway, Sweden, England, France, Italy, Spain, Denmark, Belgium, the United States, and Canada. They come from Catholic or Protestant communities. They represent the many sectarian divisions of those two Christian bodies.

Since the origin of the Christian missionary movement by the disciples of Jesus, there has arisen but one other significant missionary religion: Mohammedanism. If we accept communism as a religion (without God), then there are three. The Christian and Mohammedan religions agree upon one theological belief—that God created the world and is therefore Father to all mankind. This is the one common message that their missionary movements will carry to other peoples. From that point on, they bear little similarity. (You should have noted that Judaism and Hinduism have never been missionary religions. They are self-propagated by their own population growth. Their memberships are birthright memberships. Buddhism was a philosophy, a break-off from Hinduism. Its spread throughout the world came largely by population and trade movements of people who had made a religion out of a philosophy.)

The Christian missionary movement reveals an overwhelming desire to share with others certain values and practices that could bring peace and stability to everyday life. They had no desire to extend their faith in order to acquire an expansion of geographical territory. They did not have in mind competition for the trade markets of the world through which to improve their life-style "back home."

They endured poverty, separation from family, persecution, and martyrdom to tell of Jesus, the Nazarene, Son of God, who gave up His life to atone for the sins of mankind. Belief in Him would bring eventual salvation in a new world. Love and forgiveness were the recurrent notes in their message. Their objective was to persuade—never to compel. Acceptance or rejection of the offer were personal matters—unrelated to political governments or to racial origins.

The pace of the movement increased dramatically in the sixteenth century with the expansion of trade through the development of navigational skills. Missionaries of that time were largely of the Catholic tradition. As sectarian divisions developed within the Christian faith, following the Reformation, the pace increased further. Both Catholicism and sectarianist Protestantism reached all continents of the world.

When the Christian nations of Europe took political control of the African and American continents as colonial outposts, the missionaries were an element of the invading cultures. They reached India and the Far East. With them went western knowledge in the sciences, particularly the sciences of medicine and education. Schools, hospitals, and medical colleges went with them. By the middle of the nineteenth century their outreach was worldwide.

Inevitably the expansion of communications opened the doors also for commercial and industrial exploitation. In many of those achievements, the Christian nations can take no pride. They often represented violations of the Christian's moral codes—a testimony to man's fallibility. So it has always been in all of the world's religions.

The oft-leveled charge that Christian missionaries were a consciously consenting community in such exploitation could not be farther from the truth. They went, sacrificially, with one burden on their hearts—to share with others the Good News of the Gospel of Christ. Their efforts were supported by the voluntary financial support of their Christian associates at home. They gave generously; they extorted nothing.

By the middle of the twentieth century, despite the interruptions of World Wars I and II, missionaries from your own country, the United States of America, far outnumbered those from any other nation in the world. The Student Christian Volunteer Movement, which originated on the campuses of our colleges and universities beginning in the 1890s, persuaded thousands of young men and women to commit their lives to Christian service. As doctors, nurses, teachers, and carriers of the Good News, they fed the starving, healed the sick, and combatted illiteracy. In Christian fellowship they cooperated with their counterparts from England, Norway, Sweden, Belgium, the Netherlands—in fact, with Christian missionaries from all other countries. There were hundreds more from Canada. Finally it should be noted that hundreds of these missionaries experienced martyrdom as truly as did Paul, Peter, Mark, and Stephen.

The Islamic Missionary Movement

Six hundred years after the death of Jesus, another prophet—strikingly like those of the Old Testament—appeared in Saudi Arabia. You have learned something about him in preceding pages. Although this young Arab's life story is indeed a fascinating one and well recorded, we are more attracted to his succession of heavenly revelations during his frequent periods of trance. God, he reported, spoke to him and nominated him to be the last in the series of prophets and messenger to all mankind of God's plan for the world of human beings. Mohammed, for that was his name, had no need for an assistant like Jesus, who was but another of the false prophets clouding God's true message.

Escaping assassination and outwitting his political opponents, he launched his missionary efforts with military power. His revelations, later transcribed by his disciples, became the Koran, the bible of Islam. In it was to be found all truth. Mohammed's persuasive tool was not a gospel of love and brotherhood. It was the sword. "Accept God as interpreted to you by me or suffer the consequences!" is a fair way to paraphrase his message.

That Islam's missionary movement has been remarkably successful is written in the pages of history. Its followers stretch from the Near and Middle East across India and into the Far East. Wherever both the religion and government authority are combined, Christians are, at best, only tolerated. At times they are excluded. For one religion only is there religious freedom—that of the Koran. All others are false.

To the Christian, therefore, Mohammedanism is as exclusive as is communism. Islam's hostility toward the Jews has been mentioned. To see how history-in-the-making involves religions, follow the events in Lebanon. And while doing that, let us ask ourselves as a nation predominantly Christian as to our own position of tolerance. Where do we stand with respect to religious freedom? Since the days of our Founding Fathers we have said, "Come one; come all. We welcome you. We accept all men as brothers in love, as demonstrated by the Christ. Our life together is but the fulfillment of God's plan for all mankind." We wouldn't have it otherwise.

More than 200,000 Moslems live without interference or restriction in our fair land. With them are other religionists from every continent in the world.

When you are next in the library, ask for the latest copy of the *World Almanac*. Turn to the section which lists "Associations" —organizations of people with special interests. They are all properly listed with the government for the pursuit of their objectives. There are more than one thousand of them. From the list, we select the following. Don't skip over them lightly. As you read, ask yourselves how long such associations would be tolerated either by communism or Mohammedanism.

Atheist Association
American Atheists
Biblical Literature Society
B'nai B'rith International
Bread for the World
Brith Sholom
CORE, Congress of Racial
  Equality
CARE, Cooperative for
  American Relief Everywhere
Catholic Bishops Nat'l
  Conference
Catholic Charities
Catholic Church Extension
Catholic Daughters of America
Catholic Education Society

Catholic Extension Society
Catholic Library Ass'n.
Catholic Press Ass'n.
Catholic Rural Life Conference
Catholic War Veterans
Chaplain's Nat'l Ass'n
Christian Culture Society
Christian Endeavor Society
Christian Laity Council
Christian and Jews, Nat'l
    Conference
Church Business Administrators
Churches, World Council of
Church Women United
Civil Liberties Union
Clergy, Academy of Parish
Clinical Pastoral Educ. Ass'n
Conscious Objection Committee
Descendants of Colonial Clergy
Freedom, Young Americans for
Friends Service Committee
Gospel Music Association
Hadassah, Women Zionists
Holy Cross of Jerusalem
Human Relations Center
Human Rights and Social Justice
Jewish Appeal, United
Jewish Centers Workers' Ass'n
Jewish Committee of America
Jewish Congress of America
Jewish Federations Council
Jewish Historical Society
Jewish War Veterans
Jewish Women, Nat'l Board
Job's Daughters
Knights of Columbus
Knights Templar, USA
Liberty Lobby
Lutheran World Ministries
Ministerial Ass'n of America
Rabbinical Alliance of America
Rabbinical Assembly

Rabbis, Central Conference
Reconciliation, Conference of
Religion American Academy of
Rosicrucian Society
Separation of Church and State,
    Americans United for
Shrine, Ancient Arabic Order of
    the Nobles of the Mystic
Sons of St. Patrick
Theological Library Ass'n
Young Men's Christian Ass'n
Young Women's Christian Ass'n
Zionist Organization of America

From coast to coast, the landscape is dotted with churches, synagogues, shrines, temples, mosques, and cathedrals. Worshiping within are Moslems, Jews, Buddhists, Hindus, Catholics, and a multitude of Protestant sects: Congregationalists, Presbyterians, Plymouth Brethren, Methodists, Jehovah's Witnesses, Pentecostals, Latter-Day Saints, Seventh-Day Adventists, Baptists, and so on and on.

Disturbed, we look with great concern upon the number of young men and women who are drifting into cults of unique beliefs—seeking for something that has been slowly disappearing from our Christian families as the divorce rate has mounted—broken families with little to offer their children. Sexual intrigues, drug abuse, alcohol slavery, and the violation of children!

Statistics and polls reveal the steady increase in the "Halfway Religionists"—the Universalists, whose God still watches over them without the benefit of a saving Christ. They are no longer Christians except by a nod to acknowledge a remarkable human being. Extending the exodus from our God-centered government are increasing numbers of secular Humanists who abandon the moral judgments of a truly religious people in favor of their own ability to define the meaning of righteousness.

Despite overwhelming public opinion, our courts of justice deny the right to public prayer in our public schools and bar the presence of student activities related to religion in the extracurricular clubs and organizations. Shall the Supreme Court advise Arizona, Colorado, Florida, Ohio, and South Dakota to remove "God" from their State Seals? And follow that by removing from coin and currency "In God We Trust"? Shall we substitute a copy of Webster's Dictionary for the Bible when our elected representatives take the oath of public office? Shall we pencil-out of our founding documents all testimony to our reliance on Providence? Do these acts and words violate the rights of the Communists, Atheists, and Humanists under separation of Church from State?

Whatever import man may ascribe to "hell," it universally means evil. In short, and without profanity, we ask "What in Hell's name is going on in our fair land?" The Christian faith, nourished through 2,000 years by the Gospels proclaiming the brotherhood of all mankind, now embraces, or is embraced,by one-third of the world's population.

More than a hundred years after the founding of our nation, we established the tax-suported public schools. It had taken that long to come to the conclusion that, if we wanted a totally literate society, the general education of our children could no longer be maintained as a burden upon the church communities of the states. The system has grown by tremendous leaps and bounds as reported earlier in this study. The programs of instruction were wisely left to the responsibility of the states, with the federal government serving only in an advisory capacity. The ethnic variations within the stream of immigrants produced widely varying factors in language and background. These would have to be accommodated along with the essential instruction in languages, literature, mathematics, history and the sciences. What an opportunity for growth! Should we be surprised that our public school system early developed a morning assembly that recognized the impulse to express gratitude in prayer?

Earnestly ask your congressmen and your local school boards to permit in your school the right to hold meetings of "The Bible Club," "The Koran Club," "The Torah Club," or "The Christian Association," ouside the regular education schedule.

The Remedy

Death strikes here, and failure
Runs the length of human effort.
Famine carries off its millions
And warfare ravages a dozen lands.
Dishonesty creeps into shop and mart.
Corruption struts abroad in civic life.
Crime lets loose its terrors
Upon the unsuspecting and the innocent.

If only God could reach the hearts of men
And sensitize them to the finer things!
If evil could be brought into the light of day
Deceit would disappear, and even Death
Would lose the terror that it spreads
In human souls worldwide.
The hearts of men would throb
To cadences of song ne'er heard before,
And Nature's voice would penetrate
A glorious world where LIFE is taught
The lesson LOVE, and Heaven is the teacher.

L.R.S.
1922

Chapter XX

Epilogue

Well, what can we make of these statistics and maps? One can make much or nothing at all, depending upon his interest. This book attempts to inform America's young people of the unique political personality of their country—a nation of God-fearing people who are neither stifled nor encumbered by a governmental "church of state." From the country's founding to the present, government has been aware of "thou shalt" and "thou shalt not," a noble inheritance from Judaism. With that as a foundation, it had taken on Christianity's brotherhood-of-all-mankind, opened its doors to the oppressed and otherwise impoverished people, and through more than a century welcomed 50,000,000 immigrants to share in the new democracy. Indeed they did find here a government of, by, and for the people.

Synagogues, mosques, temples, and shrines joined Christianity's churches, cathedrals, chapels, and gospel halls. Freely they worshiped and, if they wished, promoted their particular faiths. As citizens they would vote their judgmental prejudices in secret. In amazement, the political world had watched the fledgling nation meet crisis after crisis, convict itself of its own inhumanity to man, and testify to biblically inspired acts of charity. The country's founding documents sought divine help and pledged allegiance to the Creator.

Our maturing young men and women are entitled to the truth. History cannot be taught meaningfully unless it demonstrates the inseparability of political events and religion. What this account offers is historical fact—not subjective fancy.

And now a few words of encouragement to the children of Jewish,

Moslem, Hindu, Buddhist faiths and religions other than Christian: Become involved with your own religious heritage; read your Scriptures; seek parental help in your search for truth. Your families are God-fearing people. It is America that offers you the privilege of practising and propagating your belief without governmental interference. What you ultimately come to believe with respect to a religious commitment is a very personal matter. In America, your quest for religious truth shall be your own, even its rejection. You thus have the demonstrated assurance of the Constitution of the United States that "Congress shall make no law respecting an establishment of religion or prohibiting the free exercise thereof."

Of great concern today is the rising tide of secularism whose followers maintain that all religion is but the dying remnant of primitive superstition. The concern lies not in the fear that religion will perish but that so many people may walk through a wasteland of doubt and dissent which is not America.

Ponder carefully these closing statements in verse:

Invictus

> Out of the night that covers me,
> Black as the pit from pole to pole,
> I thank whatever gods may be
> For my unconquerable soul.
>
> In the fell clutch of circumstance
> I have not winced nor cried aloud;
> Under the bludgeonings of chance
> My head is bloody but unbowed.
>
> It matters not how strait the gate,
> How charged with punishment the scroll,
> I am the master of my fate;
> I am the captain of my soul.

—William Ernest Henly

America

Oh beautiful for spacious skies,
For amber waves of grain
For purple mountain majesties
Above the fruited plain
America! America!
God shed His grace on thee
And crown thy good with brotherhood
From sea to shining sea.
Oh beautiful for pilgrim feet
Whose stern impassioned stress
A thoroughfare for freedom beat
Across the wilderness!
America! America!
God mend thine every flaw;
Confirm thy soul in self control,
Thy liberty in law.

—Katherine Lee Bates

GOD SUPREME? OR MAN SUPREME? WHERE DO YOU STAND?
IN AMERICA YOU MAY STAND WHERE YOU WISH.

THE CHOICE IS YOURS.

DATE DUE

MAR 21 2007			

Demco, Inc. 38-293

Had you been with me on that day, you would have seen the <u>RED CROSS</u> insignia giving assurance and promise of food to both the blind and the hungry.

I guess it is already past the time when Christmas greetings should be mailed, but Seventy-Years take a little more concentration! And please, if you have earlier received a copy of <u>RELIGIONS & HISTORY</u>, will you pass it on to someone else? Something tells me that it is increasingly important that we tell the children in our tax-supported schools about the impact of religion on historical development.

May you have a "Mary Christmas", rediscover your guiding star, and speak "SHALOM" to all the children of God! ·

Leslie R. Severinghaus

SEVENTY YEARS AGO when I was cycling to my English language instruction at the Peking Union Medical College in Peking, China, I snapped the photograph below. It shows hungry children looking for food "left-overs" in the collected night rubbish of that great city's inner wall.

Outside that wall, however, two "war lords" were contending for control of that ancient city before the Christian revolutionary forces of Sun Yat-Sen could replace the old dynastic posture of many centuries.

On that morning, my office windows vibrated a response to the machine-gun fire and to the occasional blast of the experimental airplane bomb. (<u>My recorded thoughts will be found on page 180. Please read them at this time.</u>)

YES, that was SEVENTY YEARS ago! The French Revolution was but a bad memory of the guillotine; Stalin is dead; Lenin sleeps in his Kremlin tomb; Hitler, hater of Jews, has been destroyed. The continent of Africa, taken over by European nations, later has surrendered to military protectorates. Thousands of once young Americans lie beneath crosses from Europe to the Far East. Vietnam continues to seek the lost, either dead or alive, and Pearl Harbor has ironically become a tourist attraction. Have you had a look at your newspaper this morning? One cannot help wondering what has gone wrong with that fabulous "mistique" called PLYMOUTH ROCK???